I0480067

SCULPTURE BOOKS FROM CRESCENT MOON PUBLISHING

The Art of Andy Goldsworthy
by William Malpas

Andy Goldsworthy: Touching Nature
by William Malpas

Richard Long: The Art of Walking
by William Malpas

The Art of Richard Long
by William Malpas

Andy Goldsworthy In Close-Up
by William Malpas

Richard Long In Close-Up
by William Malpas

Land Art In Close-Up
by William Malpas

Alison Wilding: The Embrace of Sculpture
by Susan Quinnell

Eric Gill: Nuptials of God
by Anthony Hoyland

The Erotic Object: Sexuality in Sculpture
From Prehistory to the Present Day
by Susan Quinnell

Minimal Art and Artists
by Laura Garrard

Land Art, Earthworks, Installations, Environments, Sculpture
by William Malpas

Sacred Gardens: The Garden in Myth, Religion and Art
by Jeremy Mark Robinson

Sex in Art: Pornography and Pleasure in Painting and Sculpture
by Cassidy Hughes

Postwar Art
by George Knighton

Alison Wilding

ALISON WILDING

The Embrace of Sculpture

Susan Quinnell

Crescent Moon

Crescent Moon Publishing
P.O. Box 393
Maidstone
Kent
ME14 5XU, U.K.

First published 1995. Second edition 2008.
© Susan Quinnell, 1995, 2008.

Printed and bound in Great Britain.
Set in Helvetica 10 on 15pt.
Designed by Radiance Graphics.

British Library Cataloguing in Publication data

Quinnell, Susan
Alison Wilding: Embrace of Sculpture
- (Sculptors Series)
I. Title II. Series
730.92

ISBN 1-86171-169-7
ISBN-13 9781861711694

Contents

Acknowledgements

Thanks to Karsten Schubert Ltd, London; Newlyn Orion Art Gallery, Cornwall; Tate Gallery, St Ives, Cornwall; Tate Gallery, Liverpool.

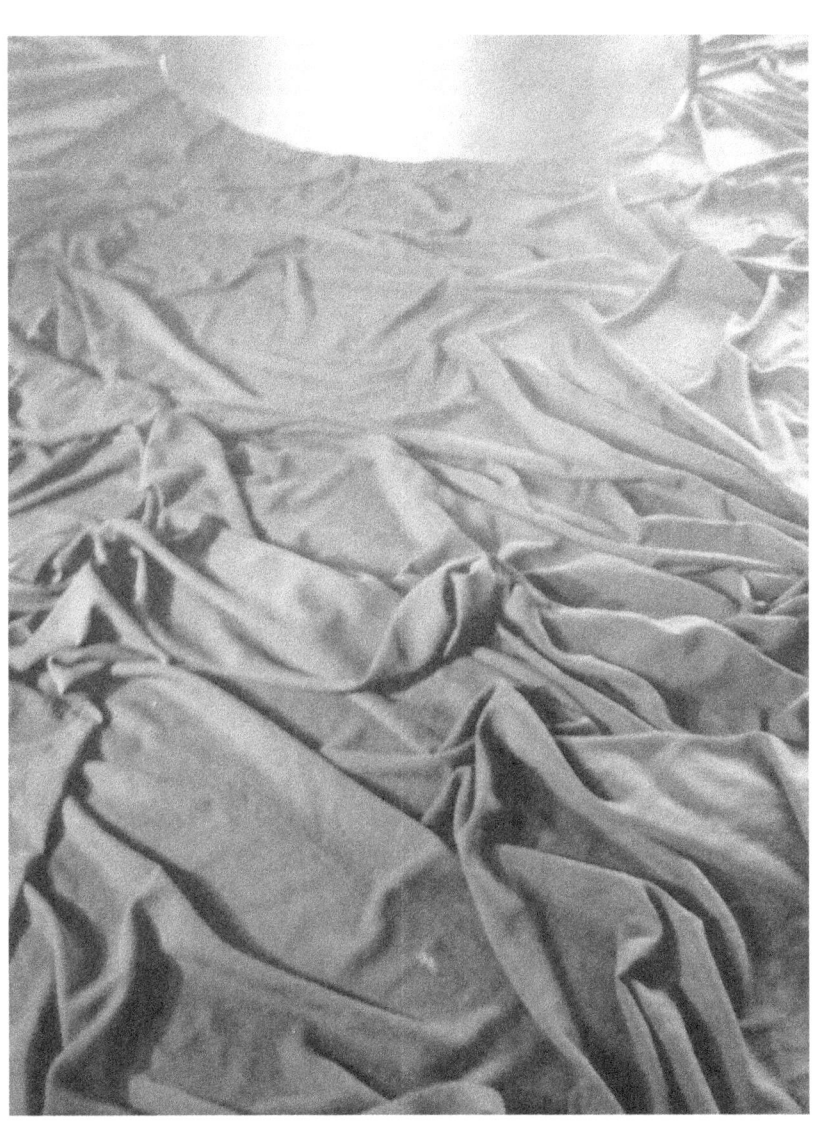

1

Introduction

Alison Wilding is one of the best sculptors around. She deserves a much wider recognition that she receives at present. Alison Wilding was born in Blackburn, Lancashire, in 1948. She went through the typical British art school education – Ravensbourne College of Art (1967-70) and the Royal College of Art (1970-73). Her one-woman shows have included Kettle's Yard Gallery, Cambridge (1982), the Serpentine Gallery, London (1985), Hirschl & Adler, New York (1989), *Bare* at Newlyn Art Gallery (1993), and a major show (*Immersion* and *Exposure*) at both the Tate Gallery, Liverpool and the Henry Moore Trust studio in Halifax (1991). She has shown new work most years since the early 1980s at her agents (Salvatore Ala Gallery, New York and Milan, and Karsten Schubert, London). Alison Wilding has participated in many of the key shows of British sculpture, such as *Figures and Objects* (Southampton, 1983); *The Sculpture Show* (Serpentine and Hayward, 1983); *The British Art Show* (Arts Council, 1984); *The British Show* (Australia, 1985); *Art and Alchemy* (Venice Biennale, 1986); *Between Object and Image* (Madrid, 1986); *Current Affairs* (Oxford, Budapest,

Prague, Warsaw, 1987); *Casting an Eye* (Cornerhouse, Manchester, 1987); *Starlit Waters* (Tate, Liverpool, 1988) and *In Site: New British Sculpture* (Oslo, 1993).

Alison Wilding's art has appeared in small group shows, such as *Eight Women Artists* (Acme, London, 1980), *Jeffrey Dennis, Alan Green, Alison Wilding* (Third Eye, Glasgow, 1986), *Domenico Bianchi, Antony Gormley, Roberto Pace, Alison Wilding* (Milan, 1986), *All That Matters: Alison Wilding, Tom Dean, Remo Salvatori, Richard Deacon* (Ontario, Saskatoon, Montreal, 1988); *Rebecca Horn, Willi Kopf, Richard Long, Alison Wilding* (Centre d'art contemporain du Domaine de Kerguehennee, 1990); *Pulsio: Louise Bourgeois, Pepe Espaliu, Alison Wilding* (Barcelona, 1991); and *Turner Prize Exhibition: Grenville Davey, Damien Hirst, David Tremlett and Alison Wilding* (Tate, London, 1992). She should have won the Turner Prize.

Alison Wilding has thus shown her sculpture with some highly valued artists: Richard Deacon, Richard Long, Louise Bourgeois, Damien Hirst and Rebecca Horn. There have been catalogues dealing with her sculpture published for one-woman shows (*Alison Wilding,* Serpentine, 1985; *Alison Wilding: Sculptures,* Karsten Schubert, 1987; *Alison Wilding: Sculptures 1987-88,* Karsten Schubert, 1988; *Alison Wilding,* Hirschl & Adler Modern, New York, 1989; *Immersion/ Exposure,* Tate, Liverpool, 1991; *Bare,* Newlyn, 1993; *Alison Wilding,* Tate, St Ives, 1994). These catalogues, though valuable, are inevitably short. I draw upon the catalogues and magazine articles, and acknowledge their important contribution towards understanding the art of Alison Wilding. This study is the first full-length analysis of Wilding's art. As Wilding's art is still developing this study cannot present a 'final' view of the artist.

There's something in Alison Wilding's sculpture which fascinates art lovers. It's difficult to say exactly what this quality of Wilding's sculpture is.

Something 'magical', perhaps, or 'mysterious', or 'erotic'. These are the sorts of terms art critics employ when they are at a loss for words. Artists such as Mark Rothko famously get this treatment (Rothko's canvases are called 'transcendent', 'sublime', 'spiritual'). John McEwen writes of Alison Wilding:

> She is pleased when her work conveys a sense of the magical, and certainly it has a powerful sense of mystery. Mysteriousness does not lend itself to description, analysis or explanation; as she herself put it to me in conversation, her pieces do not demand to be talked about. "That suggests that they do not demand to be written about either", I said. "They don't mind", she said. (59)

Penelope Curtis writes of Wilding:

> Even the smallest of her often small sculptures has tremendous and commanding presence; there is a sense of levitation in her works. (139)

As with Michelangelo, Canova, Bernini, Rodin or any of the 'great' Western sculptors, Wilding's works have enormous presence. They sit in a space with authority, like Brancusi's *Birds in Space* or Rodin's *The Kiss*.

The art historical and descriptive language of sculpture is severely impoverished, like all the descriptive languages of art. How do you describe a sound? You have terms such as timbre, tone, harmony, rhythm, pitch, and so on. But they're not enough. It's the same with colours. True, you have a few words for different kinds of blue: ultramarine, cobalt, bice, Prussian, sapphire and indigo. But look at the sky next time it's blue, and you'll find out very quickly how inadequate language is.

It's worse when we come to sculpture. The visual senses are the most highly developed in Western culture. We live in what Peter Fuller calls a 'megavisual' world.¹ But sculpture is not purely visual: it trades in touch, in texture, in volume and spatial relationships. At least sculpture has more of a vocabulary built up around it than, say, the sense of smell. But the terms available to circumscribe the forms of sculpture are pretty poor. We have basic geometric shapes and the Platonic solids: cube, tetrahedron, octahedron, icosahedron and dodecahedron, and some more complex manifestations of geometry: the Pythagorean triangle, the Golden Proportion, the *vesica piscis,* the Golden Spiral, and so on. But when we come to speak of Alison Wilding's sculpture, how do we describe her entrancing forms? There are terms such as 'cone', which might describe the 'skirted' shapes of Wilding's sculpture. But even when we go to the thesaurus for the variations on 'cone' – peak, spire, steeple, pyramid, tusk, spoke, bristle, horn, nail – we don't get any closer to Wilding's shape. The concave forms too have a number of possibilities of description, but how poor they are, really: hollow, depression, dimple, dent, trench, trough, basin, cell, valley, hole.

In a sense, it might be easy to say what Alison Wilding's is *not,* rather than what it *is.* It's not Donald Judd's Minimal boxes and ladders; it's not Alice Aycock's or Rebecca Horn's amazing, complex machines; it's not Richard Long's or Mary Miss's land art; it's not Tony Cragg's, David Mach's, Antony Gormley's, Jean-Luc Vilmouth's or Bill Woodrow's socio-ideological sculpture; it's not Richard Serra's massive steel walls; it's not Carolee Schneeman's or Annie Sprinkle's performance and body art; it's not Joseph Beuys' installations.

The sense of touch is supremely important to sculptors, as it is to most artists. Wilding speaks of its significance. Sculptors speak of the qualities of materials in terms of texture, surface, flexibility, malleability, viscosity, colour, strength, smell, associations, difficulty, and so on. Sculptors know that granite is quite a different material from steel, and certain woods – oak and holly, say – are different from pine, willow or walnut. Sculptors have a heightened 'haptic' sense, a sense of touch which involves the whole body, not just the hands. Viewers of sculptures also react to them with all the senses, not just sight. One reacts to a sculpture with the whole body. This haptic sense is

the means of touch reconsidered to include the entire body rather than merely the instruments of touch, such as the hands... It includes all those aspects of sensual detection which involve physical contact both inside and outsider the body.[2]

Bare, Alison Wilding's 1993 exhibition at Newlyn Art Gallery in Cornwall, had a catalogue to accompany the show. Emily Ash's foreword underlined the fundamental mysteriousness and ambiguity of Wilding's sculpture. 'Alison Wilding's work immediately presents the viewer with multiple possibilities of interpretation' writes Ash.[3] But *any* work by *anybody* offers 'multiple possibilities of interpretation'. In a postmodernist epoch, anything can be read in any way. The 'problem' with Wilding's sculpture is that she gives the viewer so few definite points from which to begin an appraisal. Wilding and her art affirms 'mystery', and to reach this 'mystery' requires a different set of æsthetic responses. It's not all made clear for the viewer the viewer has to make an effort in order to enjoy Wilding's art.

2

Alison Wilding and Other Sculptors

Sculpture is a three dimensional projection of primitive feeling: touch, texture, size and scale, hardness and warmth, evocation and compulsion to move, live and love.

Barbara Hepworth[1]

Alison Wilding is one of the most erotic of contemporary female sculptors. She is also one of the very few women sculptors in Britain who are spoken of highly, and is regarded by some as approaching the status of such luminaries of the sculpture world as Barry Flanagan, Richard Long, Anish Kapoor, Tony Cragg, David Nash and Bill Woodrow. But Wilding's sculpture stands alone. No one else is making work like hers, as Fenella Crichton writes:

> Her work is impossible to categorise because she has created her own sculptural language, which is special to her, and which does separate her from the new wave of British sculpture... Like Eva Hesse, Wilding's language is in large part the result of her passionate involvement with the materials she uses. Whether brass,

silk, copper, or wax, she works with their pliability and texture in order to bring out the most secretive and sensuous aspects of their nature.[2]

Most of the 'feminist' art being produced today is by women. Male artists have only made tentative steps in producing art that radically questions or rewrites patriarchal attitudes, values, ideas, experiences or laws. Much of 'feminist' or 'women's' art celebrates the 'feminine', what is special to 'femininity' or 'womanhood', the being of 'woman' and women.

Some male critics and masculinist/ patriarchal criticism cannot accept a life for feminist art outside of masculinist/ patriarchal art/ society. The problem is, partly, one of æsthetics and criticism: that is, is there a true 'feminist' æsthetics and criticism? Is there really 'women's art'?, because an authentic 'women's'/ 'female' art would require a 'women's'/ 'female' æsthetic theory to make it work. Thus, for masculinist/ patriarchal art theory, 'women's'/ 'feminist art' cannot exist without masculinist/ patriarchal art theory. Lodged so deeply in masculinist/ patriarchal art theory, 'women's'/ 'feminist art' cannot extricate itself. To simplify this argument, it would mean that Alison Wilding's sculpture (or Louise Bourgeois', or Rebecca Horn's, or Nancy Graves', or Alice Aycock's, or Mary Miss's, or Jo Spence's, or Susan Hiller's, or Annie Sprinkle's) could not exist on its own, without being linked to male artists/ masculinist/ patriarchal æsthetics. Simplistically speaking, Alison Wilding's work cannot be discussed as 'women's art', but only as art working within a masculinist/ patriarchal society and tradition.

Many women sculptors have explored 'feminine' imagery. Louise Bourgeois explored the relations between form and eroticism, volume and psychology, shape and Nature. Her forms are nearly always dealing with eroticism – her *Nature Study*, for instance, feature those bulbous volumes which are practically her trademark, echoing breasts, clitorises, vulvas, buttocks, heads, hands, knees, tongues, all the parts of the eroticized body.

Wilding's contemporary, Andy Goldsworthy, employs 'feminine' shapes and motifs, such as the vulva. Upstairs at his 1994 exhibition *Herd of Arches* in London, was a stone with a vulva-shape carved out of it. The opening was in layers, receding into the stone, so that the effect was distinctly labial, suggesting the inner folds of the vagina and womb. For Peter Gabriel's 1992 album *Us*, Goldsworthy created a vulvic shape out of twigs, set in some mossy rocks. Richard Long also speaks in gendered terms of his lines and circles: the lines are 'male things', while the circles and water are 'a sort of female'.[3]

Among male sculptors, the eroticism of Andy Goldsworthy's and Richard Long's sculpture is of a different order from traditional, figurative sculpture, the sculpture of Michelangelo and Bernini. Due to the abstract nature of Long's and Goldsworthy's sculpture, their work generally escapes obvious sexism. We know about the famous sexist and heterosexist depictions of people in sculpture. They include Alberto Giacometti's *Spoon Woman*, a view of woman as Earth Mother, a totemic figure; Gaston Lachaise's *Standing Woman*, one of those smooth, curvy Goddess types, also favoured by Maillol; Hans Bellmer's bizarre Dolls, where the slit of a vulva is where the head would be, and set amidst exaggerated, bulbous forms; Gaudier-Breska's *Red Stone* Dancer, though it attempts a new way of depicting gesture and posture in space, is still sexist; Elie Nadelman's *Dancer*, like Paul Manship's *Dancer and Gazelles*, and Degas' *Dancer* sculptures, is also sexist; and Kirchner's *Standing Nude* is pornography masquerading as art, but then, most of his depictions of women are pornography. British sculptor Peter Randall-Page (b. 1954) produces, like Jean Arp, softly rounded forms which have affinities with Alison Wilding's works. In particular, Randall-Page's *Untitled* (1980), which looks like a spiral shell, and his *Nocturne II* (1979, both outdoors at Milton Keynes) are Wildingian.

Other sculptors, or sculptures, which have affinities with Alison Wilding's work include John Newling's *The Rapi Plough* (1983), a series of objects including Wildingian spirals and vulva-shape volumes. Nicholas Pope produces forms that echo Wilding's: Pope's works are softly rounded, like some of William Tucker's, and most of Louise Bourgeois' pieces. Some of Pope's outdoor works are large, such as *The Arch* (1985). It is the arch itself that fascinates Pope, for the arch is such an elegant structure. Pope's *The Arch* is dove-tailed and pegged together, made from two young trees and one mature tree. Pope was consciously trying to make a work with oak, not just with any wood. 'I wanted to make an oak-wood arch not an arch made from wood.' (in Strachan, 70) More like Alison Wilding's work, are Pope's boulders and small scale pieces. Like Carl Andre, Nicholas Pope has placed large stones in an urban environment. Andre's *Stone Field* is one of his site-specific works of the 70s, consisting of 26 very large glacial boulders. It is an imposing piece, introducing the idiosyncratic, organic shapes of Nature into the 'geometric wilderness' (D.M. Thomas's term) of the city. Pope's *Three Wilderness Stones* (1980, Southampton) and *Five Amorphous Shapes* are huge boulders of Forest of Dean stone in humanmade environments. Pope's stones spread out across parkland or the forecourts of modern business complexes, bringing the organic, idiosyncratic forms of Nature into the angular, linear environment of the city. Like Barbara Hepworth and Andy Goldsworthy, like poets such as Peter Redgrove and Rainer Maria Rilke, Nicholas Pope is fascinated by stones. Hepworth loved the white granite rounded stones of West Penwith, and put them in her studio in St Ives. It's easy to see how some of Hepworth's sculptures took part of their inspiration from the beautiful granite boulders of Cornwall. Hepworth spoke lovingly of Cornwall, and Wilding has also been moved by the Cornish landscape. In the article in *The Studio* (1946) Hepworth wrote:

I have gained very good inspiration from the Cornish land- and sea-scape, the horizontal line of the sea and the quality of light and colour which reminds me of the Mediterranean light and colour which so excites one's sense of form; and first and last there is the human figure which in the country becomes a free and moving part of a greater whole. (Witzling, 280)

Some of Richard Deacon's forms recall Wilding's sculptures. Deacon's *Tooth and Claw* (1986) brings two materials together (steel and carpet), as so often in Wilding. The curvy shapes of Deacon's work recall Wilding's *Nature: Blue and Gold*. Deacon has spoken of the 'poetic' in sculpture, a concern central to Wilding's art: poetry, says Deacon, has a 'surface obviousness with underlying depth' which is 'similarly found in sculpture'.[4] In sculptors such as Deacon, Stephen Cox, Anish Kapoor, Rachel Whiteread, Shirazeh Houshiary, Boyd Webb, Antony Gormley and Wilding the poetic or rmetaphoric is important.

Important contemporary women sculptors include Nancy Graves, Eva Hesse, Niki de Sant-Phalle, Mary Miss, Rebecca Horn, Eva Hesse and Louise Nevelson. Eva Hesse is particularly powerful. Critics have noted the affinities between Eva Hesse and Alison Wilding. Hesse's artworks have immediate impact, and they are challenging. They hang from ceilings, in rows, or squat on the floor in clusters (as in *Repetition 19, III*) made of rubber, latex, cloth, wire, fibreglass, evoking organic forms in ambivalent, sensual ways.[5] Pieces such as *Ingeminate* offer up a mysterious affirmation of life in the form of two coils of cord connected by a long piece of surgical hose. Sans II, meanwhile, is a dozen rectangular 'compartments' made from fibreglass which hints at some obscure systematization of flesh and organic form.[6] Hesse wrote: '[i]f I can name the content...it's the total absurdity of life.'[7] Hesse's *Repetition 19, III* (1968) is a group of fibreglass cylinders, each 12 inches high. Like Wilding's *Veiled No. 2* (1993), Hesse's works are opaque, the fibreglass offering a peculiar kind of yellowy luminosity.

Hesse's art unsettles traditional notions of sculpture, with its semi-permanent materials, its soft, pliant materials. Hesse does away with the hard-edged materialism of Minimalism, and goes beyond the solid, firm sculptures of the past which employed hard materials such as bronze, stone and steel. Hesse's hanging, rubbery forms suggest biological and organic processes, of birth, growth and decay, of transience and impermanence. For the male critic, they are disturbing: '[o]ften they seem like dream visions of intimate parts pendulous breasts or yawning vaginas – so that simple, dangling strings suggest umbilical cords or streaming milk.'[8] Patriarchal art criticism is unable to deal fully with the dynamics of women's art, it seems, so it denigrates it, dismisses it as 'vulva art', as Robert Hughes called Judy Chicago's work. Hesse speaks in Romantic, emotional terms of her art, employing words such as 'essence' and 'soul'. She speaks of wanting to emphasize 'soul or presence or whatever you want to call it.' Although Alison Wilding is not as openly emotional in her descriptions of her art, these words of Hesse's could apply, with some minor revisions, to Wilding's art:

> I think art is a total thing. A total person giving a contribution. It is an essence, a soul...In my soul art and life are inseparable.[9]

Jackie Winsor made the Minimal cube one of her major forms, but she made her cubes richly textured, from 'natural' materials, such as twine and wood.[10] Winsor's cubes take the Minimal cube only as a starting point, because her series of cubes are explorations of the mysteries of being. They are objects of yearning and poignancy.[11] They are not the slick, smooth cubes of fibreglass and steel of Donald Judd, Sol LeWitt and Robert Morris. Some of Winsor's works change or decay: the *Burnt Piece* cube burnt away, alchemically, when the artist fired its interior. As with the land artists, Winsor said: 'I was unable to see how the piece would look until the moment of completion.'[12] Alison Wilding also has a sculpture made from burnt materials, called *Burned*. A pair of wooden structures were covered with a dense web of copper wire. The wood was then burnt away, leaving the two copper structures left. The process of making the sculpture, always important to Wilding, was made explicit In *Burned*. The two structures spoke of their formation and past, a ceremonial fire.

Louise Nevelson produced huge reliefs or structures which are like Cubist or Constructionist altarpieces full of objects, various articles made of wood, all painted in one colour, black, white or gold: chair legs, railings, door knobs. Her sculptures are like magical cupboards, vertical dreamscapes made of boxes stacked on top of each other. They recall Joseph Cornell, but every object is united by the single colour, while in Cornell objects retain their individuality, and specialness to the sculptor.

The extravagant art of contemporary land artists is well-known: Walter de Maria with his kilometre-long brass rod buried in the ground and his *Lightning Field*, Michael Heizer who took chunks out of the American desert, Christo who 'wrapped' buildings, bridges and coasts, Robert Smithson with his mythic *Spiral Jetty*. Alison Wilding has only a distant affinity with the 1960s land artists. Their art is vast in scale, aiming to overpower the viewer. Wilding's art, meanwhile, has quite different aims. Sixties Minimalists, such as Carl Andre, Donald Judd, Dan Flavin, Robert Morris and Brice Marden, were important for sculpture. Wilding clearly develops the Minimalists' sense of the object, of objecthood, of presence. One can see how Alison Wilding's art is founded on some 60s and Minimal principles: Wilding's sculpture is set on the floor, for instance, which Robert Morris thought important. Putting the works on the floor, though, places them in the same space as the viewer. There is a different kind of intimacy between the viewer and the art object when it's on the floor. Instead of looking up to the sculpture, on its pedestal, it's in the same space as the viewer. Wilding's sculpture also requires a lot of space around the works. This is nothing new: for a long time sculptors have been acutely aware of the way their works are exhibited. Many sculptors have used the space of the room or exhibition environment in their works.

The Minimal world was clean, calm, devoid of unruliness, violence, even ambiguity. Something like an airport: white, spotless, spacious. Or a new shopping mall. A row of pristine supermarket shelves, stacked high with new cans of fruit, the labels all turned face-out. Minimal art is an art for the commodity-rich 1960s, where mass production created a uniformity to the appearances of so much of street, home, personal, medical, transport and educational furniture. Minimal sculpture, Barbara Rose remarked, looks 'machine-made, industrial, standardized, materialized or stamped out as a whole'.[13] Other aspects of Minimal sculpture include the multiplicity of sculptural material (fluorescent lights, plexiglass, fibre-glass, Formica, chrome, plastic), simplicity, surface, and the insistence on the environment and contextual space. Minimal sculptures are not set on pedestals, like Renaissance or Greek sculpture; they sit on the floor, or lean against walls (as in Robert Morris' *Floor Piece*, or Carl Andre's *Cedar Piece*). Minimalist sculptures exist in the same space, on the same plane (the floor) as the viewer. They are, as Robert Morris said, in an in-between cultural space, somewhere between being monuments and being ornaments, between being architecture and jewellry.[14] In Minimal sculpture, surfaces are, typically, smooth, utterly smooth and 'pure'. Simplicity is exalted, as is repetition, seriality, process, flatness as well as volume and space. The many materials are flattened out and depersonalized, and gestures, so important to certain kinds of sculpture, such as that of Michelangelo, are suppressed. Indeed, the flatness of the surfaces, whether in Robert Morris, Donald Judd, Dan Flavin, Carl Andre, Ronald Bladen or Tony Smith, is crucial, and some commentators call Minimal sculpture 'boring'.[15] For Peter Fuller, there is nothing 'spiritual' about Minimal art: he speaks of 'the numbing vacuity of works by artists such as Carl Andre, Agnes Martin, Ellsworth Kelly or Brice Marden.' (xxxv) The boringness, though, becomes a part of the metaphysics of Minimal sculpture, so that Lucy Lippard writes: '[t]he exciting thing about... the "cool" artists is their daring challenge of the concepts of boredom, monotony and repetition... their demonstration that intensity does not have to be melodramatic.'[16] And Judd said about the charge of reductionism:

> I object to the whole reduction idea. If my work is reductionist, it's because it doesn't have the elements that people thought should be there. But it has other elements that I like.[17]

Boring art for some is exhilarating art for others, just as erotic art for some is pornography for others. Thus, James Mellow wrote that a Donald Judd show was 'one of the most provocative of the season',[18] while Barbara Rose described Judd's art as 'our most radical sculpture, if not perhaps our fullest'.[19] Certainly Judd's wall reliefs are beautiful, especially when made in brass or copper. Judd combined the sensuality of these industrial materials with cool geometric patterns. Judd, like other Minimal sculptors, combined austerity with sensuality, producing 'minimal forms at the service of glamorous, hedonistic effects of light' (Hilton Kramer).[20] As Barbara Haskell writes:

> By coupling these luxurious materials with spare forms, he exploited their inherent "language". The opposition between the inert and rigorous geometry of his forms, and the opulent hedonism and shimmering color effects of his surfaces accounted for the unexpectedly exultant lyricism of his work.[21]

The bombastic, 'monumental', massive and brash 3-D art of contemporary sculpture was not made exclusively by male artists. Mary Miss created a 5-acre scale work in Illinois,[22] while Nancy Holt produced gigantic *Sun Tunnels*, 18ft long pipes that were 9 feet high with many holes punched in the side, to let light in.[23] Nancy Holt's art, with its large, heavy landscaping gestures (such as her *Dark Star Park*), is comparable with the male 'earth artists'. The globes and pools of water, though, are traditional 'feminine' volumes, here given a new, monumental turn. Helen Escobedo has created some huge concrete and steel sculptures which 'attempt to fuse hard-edge geometric forms with nature's organic manifestations' as she puts it. Works such as *Snake* rise impressively from the Earth, celebrating the flux and movement of organic forms. Beverly Pepper's large, curving mirrored slabs of wood buried in sandy beaches might be seen as a type of 'Earth Mother art', art which worships and works with the Earth, rather than, as in so much of male 'land art', cutting or penetrating it, phallically (like Michael Heizer, Robert Smithson and Waler de Maria). Wilding's art also has affinities with the Italian Arte Povera ('poor art') movement, with its insistence on simple, organic materials (soil, grass, fire, wood, wax). The Arte Povera artists (Jannis Kounellis, Mario Merz, Giovanni Anselmo) brought unadorned (though not unmanipulated) 'natural' materials into the gallery, which produced a different sort of æsthetic shock: fluffy cotton packed into a steel enclosure; an igloo made from broken glass, slate, clay, wax and branches; a piece of lettuce bound to a chunk of granite. Like de Maria filling a gallery with soil, Kounellis brought Nature (some horses) into a gallery in Rome. The horses stabled in the white, modern gallery provided a striking contrast between Nature and culture, the animal and the man-made worlds.

Rebecca Horn's sculptures, like her mentor's Beuys' works, are based (like Alison Wilding's) on natural forms, but also on movement, dance, time and environments. Horn's assemblages of feathers, cogs, rods and levers startle with their time delayed movements. Her works spit, flutter, leak, wave and tilt. Her works come from a melancholy, mnemonic attitude, and speak of fundamental feelings: death, loneliness, love, pain, ambiguity.[24] Horn creates guns that spit blood (*High Moon*), upside down pianos that disgorge their entrails (*Concert For Anarchy*), and clusters of binoculars that swivel round to peer at the viewer (*Forest of the Blindfolded Singers*). Horn's wonderful *Peacock Machine* is an exuberant activator of space, one of those pieces that aims for the essence of a natural form and captures it: a peacock's magnificent tail.[25] Except Horn's peacock's tail slowly unfolds barbed javelins. It was Brancusi's task to strip away the detritus that had accumulated around sculpture, Henry Moore said, and to give us the pure, simple shape. What Brancusi did was 'to concentrate on very simple shapes, to keep his sculpture, as it were, one-cylindered, to refine and polish a single shape to a degree almost too precious.'[26] This is what many contemporary sculptors have done, keeping their shapes simple and purified: Richard Long, Eva Hesse, Alison Wilding, Andy Goldsworthy, David Nash, Richard Serra, Stepen Cox, Peter Randall-Page, Donald Judd and Robert Smithson.

BARBARA HEPWORTH AND ALISON WILDING

Barbara Hepworth is a direct ancestor or perhaps partly an inspiration of Wilding's sculpture. Hepworth's organic forms, as with Brancusi, hover between subjectivity and objectivity, between natural form and æsthetic abstraction (as in her *Two Forms*, for example.) Like Brancusi, Hepworth maintained that she always returned to Nature, and took her inspiration from Nature. For her, Nature meant the (Cornish) landscape, and the human body, and the symbiotic and tender relationship between the two. 'We return always to the human form – the human form in landscape' she said. Her sculpture stems from emotion and expression, from feeling: 'I rarely draw what I see – I draw what I feel in my body' she stated.[27] Hepworth's distinctive forms, with their smooth curves and holes, are clearly sensual objects. Hepworth acknowledged the sensuality of sculptural forms.

The links between Barbara Hepworth and Alison Wilding are worth pursuing: Hepworth's pierced forms, for example, have affinities with Wilding's holed forms. For Hepworth, the pierced hole created a new sense of the relationship between inner and outer, and between the viewer and the sculpture. The piercing of the sculptural form opened up 'an infinite variety of continuous curves in the third dimension' ("Approach to Sculpture", Witzling, 279). Wilding has similarly explored the relation between inside and outside with her holed sculptures. What Hepworth has to say about the relationship of two forms also applies to Alison Wilding's sculpture: Hepworth sees the two forms as having an organic, symbiotic relationship, like mother and child. The maternal metaphor is absolutely apposite for Wilding's poetry of nurturance and embrace. Hepworth speaks of 'the tender relationship of one living thing beside another...the repose of say a mother and child, or the feeling of the embrace of living things'; Hepworth speaks of the harmony of inner and outer being like 'a nut in its shell or a child in the womb' (*A Pictorial Autobiography*, in Witzling, 285). This image, of the nut in its shell, like the child in the womb or the clitoris nestling amongst the labia, is, as we shall see, an apposite metaphor for Alison Wilding's sculpture of embrace.

Another female sculptor in the Hepworth mould is Naomi Blake (b. 1924). Blake combines abstract and figurative elements, often with a religious theme. As with Alison Wilding, Naomi Blake is much concerned with the interrelationship of two main elements, often with an undercurrent of nurturing themes. Blake has produced figures inside an oval shape, such as her *Refugee*, sited outside Bristol cathedral (1981). The oval shape is clearly an echo of the mediæval *vesica piscis*, that vulva/ womb shape found in mediæval and Renaissance art. In the *mandorla* or *vesica piscis* Christ ascended to Heaven after the Resurrection, as did the Virgin Mary at Her Assumption. The Virgin Mary often appeared in a vesica piscis in Renaissance art: Naomi Blake revives the tradition, placing a mother and child inside a large (7 ft) fibreglass vesica piscis (at Norwich cathedral, 1984). Similarly, Alison Wilding produces nurturing images: her sculptures often consist of one large form sheltering another smaller element. Another

32

Naomi Blake sculpture, in Highgate, north London, has more obvious affinities with Alison Wilding's work: *Blake's Image* (1979) is another oval, more explicitly vulvic in shape. At the top of the oval is a spherical object. The effect of the globe recessed in the vulvic shape directly recalls the clitoris and vulva.

Lila Katzen sets alive public spaces with her flowing, curling forms.[29] Alice Aycock, using science as her Muse, has produced some wonderfully fantastical machines, such as *The Angels Continue Turning the Wheels of the Universe*, or the marvellous, massive piece *The Miraculous Machine in the Garden (Tower of the Winds)*, which features 268 antenna and bells ringing in a vacuum.[30] In sculpture, it seems, more than in painting, one can carve out a niche for oneself: Aycock's incredible machines with their equally incredible titles (*One Thousand and One Nights in the Mansion of Bliss*) are absolutely her own. Only Tinguely is close to Aycock, or perhaps Rebecca Horn. Aycock speaks of desiring to activate poetry and fantasy in her sculpture, and her amazing inventions do that. Any work that has bells ringing in a vacuum is clearly the product of someone with a vivid imagination. Like Robert Stackhouse's *Running Animals, Reindeer Way*, Richard Serra's *Olson* or Judy Pffaf's *N.Y.C.-B.Q.E.*, Aycock's machines dominate their environment. There is not much space for the viewer. Alison Wilding's sculptures activate space in very different way. Her sculptures do not 'dominate' a gallery, as Richard Serra's massive, heavy thirty-six foot long steel slabs do. Wilding's sculptures do not envelop or overwhelm the viewer, like Christo's wrapped buildings or Joseph Beuys' felt room installations. Wilding's sculptures sit quietly on the floor or against a wall. They are 'human' scale, but all art is 'human-scale' (made by humans, therefore always in relation to humans). More correctly, Wilding's pieces are a 'manageable' size, a few feet long or wide or high, objects that can be handled by one person. The quietness and compactness, the self-sufficiency and 'small' scale of Wilding's art is the opposite of the massive gestures of

Christo, Heizer, Beuys, Miss, Escobedo or Moore. At the same time, Wilding's sculptures do tend to fill up a space, as the British sculptor Richard Deacon noted:

> Recently talking with her in her studio, I remarked that there seemed to be no neutral ground, no safe distance, in relation to her sculpture. However far or near you get, the sculpture always takes up the space you give it.

Miriam Shapiro has taken up materials branded 'feminine' by patriarchy (cotton, taffeta, burlap, wool, sequins, buttons, thread) and has created artworks (she calls them 'femmages') that deal with notions of the home, feminist iconography, abstraction and the æsthetics of 'Pattern and Decoration'. Shapiro says: 'I wanted to explore and express a part of my life which I had always dismissed – my homemaking, my nesting'.[31] A number of male artists have explored traditionally 'feminine' notions of pattern, decoration and colour, among them Robert Zakanitch, Lucas Samaras, Robert Kushner, Rodney Ripps, Kim MacConnel, Frank Stella and Ned Smyth. But it is women artists who make the most flamboyant and intricate artworks in these areas, such as Joyce Kozloff or Valerie Jaudon. The 'traditional' 'women's' arts and crafts of textiles, pattern, sewing, decoration, pottery, etc, are bound up with the economies of labour, race, class, identity, patriarchy, politics and finance. They are modes of production and art that are regarded as secondary by patriarchal culture, not as 'high art', such as painting or sculpture. The economics of artistic production are embedded with patriarchal slants, just as much as the images themselves. The piece of textiles, the decorative tile, the pot, are objects that in the patriarchal system speak of their second-rate mode of production. As Catherine King writes, '[m]edia associated with 'malestream' codes, like bronze, marble, or oil, have been regarded with suspicion' by women artists.[32] Although Goldsworthy uses impermanent materials such as leaves and snow, he also uses traditional, 'masculine' media such as stone. This helps his art to be regarded as 'high', 'serious' art.

34

One aspect of 'feminist' or 'women's' art is embodied by the figure of the Goddess, the ancient and primæval Great Mother of all, celebrated then – and now – as Isis, Ishtar, Demeter, Kali, etc. The Goddess is now variously interpreted as fact, experience, idea, æsthetic, cult, religion, pagan emblem and many other things by women artists. There are a host of artists who have made what we might call 'Goddess art', art that employs the figure of the Goddess as an embodiment of female being or experience. Judy Chicago, Mary Beth Edelson, Miriam Shapiro, Niki de Sant-Phalle, Louis Bourgeois, Helen Chadwick.

Mary Beth Edelson engages in the resurgence of the Goddess, in her *Great Goddess* series. Edelson has also produced a piece on menstruation, entitled, appropriately, *Blood Mysteries*. In a piece of performance art, Catherine Elwes sat in an enclosed studio space and menstruated.[33] Judy Chicago, mentioned above, looked to the flowers of Georgia O'Keeffe, which, she said, 'stand for femininity'.[34]

Niki de Sant-Phalle has produced exuberant Goddesses, such as her *Black Venus*, or her marvellous *Pink Childbirth*, a Great Mother Goddess made from dolls, toys, tissues and various items collected together like a totem of the prehistoric world, while Sant-Phalle's *Un Ensemble de "Les Nanas"* is an effervescent – and multicoloured – representation of female forms, dancing, cavorting, balancing.[38] Among non-figurative, abstract or partially-figurative artists, women such as Nancy Graves are absolutely astonishing, with her superb multi-media constructions.[35] Nancy Graves' skeletal, fossil-like works combine fantasy and natural forms in 'one exuberantly open-form, polychrome, freestanding construction after another' (D. Wheeler, 303).

Shirazeh Houshiary, who exhibited with Wilding at Kettle's Yard Gallery in

Cambridge in early 1982, also stressed the poetic, metaphoric nature of sculpture. 'My quest is to unfix the image,' Houshiary said, 'to go beyond the materiality of things.'[37] Houshiary's statement of intent recalls, again, Brancusi's project of trying to reach the 'essence of things'. Houshiary's abstract morphologies reflect those of Alison Wilding: in sculptures such Houshiary's *Himma* (1985, Lisson Gallery) mystery is stressed as Houshiary unpacks form, trying to approach what is underneath. Her work is about the dialectic of inner and outer form, 'a way of fragmenting the whole' across the horizontal (as against the 'fixed' symmetry of the vertical format). 'My quest is to perceive the dialogue between the hidden and the visible' says Houshiary (ib.), a goal which Wilding echoes in her sculpture.

The body features occasionally in the art of Andy Goldsworthy, Antony Gormley and Richard Long. We see the grass rubbed flat by Long's feet, or the shape of Goldsworthy's body after a snowfall, or Gormley's body impressed in sliced bread. And Long and Goldsworthy occasionally appear in photographs, beside their work. We see Goldsworthy's hands, and other parts of the sculptor, but there is nothing in Long's and Goldsworthy's work that is as ferocious as feminist and women's body and performance art. Feminist artists use the body to explore political, erotic, pornographic, æsthetic and philosophical discourses. As Lisa Tickner writes: '[l]iving *in* a female body is different from looking *at* it, as a man. Even the Venus of Urbino menstruated, as women know and men forget.'[38] The female nude, for so long the model and image and object of lust in so many 'high art' paintings, has usurped the power relation between artist and art object, and between artwork and spectator. The woman is no longer content to be looked at and lusted after: she is making her own art, employing her body in a radical, challenging way. The 'Old Master/ *Playboy* tradition', as Tickner calls it, has been smashed.[39]

Feminist body and performance art is a way of repossessing the body, sexuality, identity, power, it is a way of 'rewriting the body'. It can be an act of transgression and subversion, which usurps the power relation between spectator and artwork, so that the (male) viewer's 'cloak of invisibility has been stripped away and his spectatorship becomes an issue within the work' as Catherine Elwes puts it. (Elwes, op.cit., 172) Carolee Schneemann pulls a scroll from her vagina and reads from it.[40] Chila Kumari Burman makes 'body prints'. Karen Finley pours 'a can of yams over her naked buttocks'; she is 'a frightening and rare presence'.[42] In her *Cut Off Balls* she castrates Wall Street bankers.[41] Mary Duffy displays her disabled body in performance and photographic sequences;[43] Jo Spence has photographed the 'unhealthy and ageing female body'.[44]

3

The Alchemy of Forms

Alchemy is a philosophy of relationships, and is very much founded on the body, on organic processes, on the invisible mysteries made visible, just as in Alison Wilding's work. Wilding's work, like alchemy, continually points toward transmutation, at the process of changing from one state to another, one substance to another. Always in alchemy the *physical* is stressed, *and* the spiritual. Alchemy always speaks of working with real liquids, real stones, real heat and real vessels. It is a 'science', one of the mediæval sciences, has its systems, its methodologies, where the processes are logged and collaborated. Similarly, sculpture is a very physical activity ('sculture is the reaction of a *real object* said Barbara Hepworth [Witzling, 285]). Yet, at the same time, just like sculpture, alchemy is not only physical, it has a spiritual dimension. In alchemy, the physical is an expression of the spiritual, the physical world is where the spiritual is manifested. It is the same for art as for alchemy: viewers see in art the manifestation of something sublime, sacred, mysterious, divine, as well as all sorts of other things. Alchemy, for C.G. Jung, was a potent source of symbolism, and one can ruminate for hours on the symbolism of sculpture.

Sculpture, though wholly 'physical', has a spiritual dimension. In transforming matter, the sculptor, like the alchemist, hopes for a reaction on a higher plane. Critics talk of the psychological, æsthetic, social, ideological and mythic aspects of art: certainly Wilding, like many artists, declines to be speak of the exact effects she is striving for. She will not say exactly what responses she'd like from her work. An artist has to take whatever responses are forthcoming. A decent response, anyway, is rare: most artists work in isolation, and seldom find a like-minded soul with whom to exchange views. As she won't say precisely what her æsthetic intentions are, we can muse that alchemical affinities are part of Wilding's intentions. Besides, whatever the artist's intentions might be, the viewer is free to come up with whatever connotations s/he likes. Always we return to the inherent *mysteriousness* of Alison Wilding's art. It's not as obvious as, say, Canova or Michelangelo. So the alchemical connection might be grasping wildly at the wrong sort of connections.

Symbolic connections made obvious in Wilding's sculpture include the notion of the egg (so important to Constantin Brancusi). The egg needs no gloss as a symbol of life, of birth, of motherhood and nurturance, of the womb, and so on. Other Wildingian symbols include the cone, seen in many sculptures (not always a 'pure' witch's hat cone; the sculptures *Dismantle*, *Fugue* and *Veiled* offer altered cones). A central nodule or globe surrounded by a thin metal collar or cradle is another favourite motif (in *Well*, *Brim*). There is the circle, used in many sculptures (*Pond*, *Untitled*). The hollow appears in pieces such as *Into the Dark*: the more one studies the symbols in Wilding's art, the shapes and motifs and patterns she employs, one realizes that so much of it relates to the symbolism of the feminine. There are so many hollows, vessels, caves, holes, so many shapes that echo vases, bowls, caverns, all symbols of the vulva, the womb, the mother, the feminine. Here in a Jungian, Marie-Louise von Franz, on (alchemical) vessels:

> The vessel is the womb of the Mother Church, the uterus, and so it has a definite feminine maternal quality.

Von Franz goes on to compare the Christian church to a vessel, a way of holding and keeping religious feelings. Psychologically, though, von Franz writes that

> the vessel with vows, ideas, basic feelings, and concepts which we try to hold together and keep from escaping in life, for the vessel can hold these things so that they are not lost. It therefore constitutes a means of becoming conscious. (ib., 28)

Wilding does not make dogmatic the maternal, feminine discourses of her sculptural vessels. It's clear, though, that the sheer number of vessels in her art show her to be exploring the related discourses of the unconscious, maternity, parent-children relationships and emotions.

The history of alchemy is the history of mysterious vessels or containers of many kinds. One shape recurs continually; the globe or egg-shape. In alchemical treatises, this is the shape that keeps on cropping up. It is also the shape that Wilding uses again and again. In the alchemical vessels depicted in the theoretical books of alchemy, we see fires being conjured, dragons being burnt, trees growing, the king and queen of alchemy copulating, worlds forming and imploding. Fire is absolutely central to the processes of alchemy. It is in the fire that many of alchemy's transformations take place. Wilding has used fire in an allusive, poetic fashion in her sculpture. There are pieces such as *Vestal* and *Her Furnace*, which refer to fire. The sculpture *Burned* was created by fire, using one of the alchemical materials, copper.

As with Joseph Cornell's boxes, the alchemical egg-shaped vessel is a container in which anything might happen. It is a cosmos in miniature. In Brancusi's work, the egg-shape has a cosmological significance. It is a mini-universe, and speaks of the birth of worlds. In Alison Wilding's sculpture, the egg-shape is not given such obvious religious/ symbolic connotations. They are there, though. In *Blue Skies*, for instance, there is a largish stone at the centre of the work (a piece of Cornish granite – one finds these globes of granite on many beaches in Cornwall, rubbed smooth by the tide). In amongst the flat, rigid, angular metal structures the softly rounded stone stands out. As with the other Wilding works, the metal flats seem to be nurturing the stone; at the same time, however, the stone brings alive the sculpture. As so often, Wilding deftly teases out the properties of materials, emphasizing similarities and differences so eloquently. Set next to metal, Wilding's stones seem even more 'stone-like': they offer a different kind of strength and rigidity from metal. Another stone-and-metal sculpture is *Brim* (1984), where a largish oval piece of granite is set in a steel holder like an egg in an egg cup. Either side of the egg-shaped stone is a wide, thin 'collar', a sweep of steel that curves gently upwards, as if to protect the stone.

Well (1985) is a wall version of the Wilding motif of a central nodule or globe and a curved cradle. Wilding loves softly curved pieces of thin steel (they appear in *Brim*, *Vestal*, *Immersion*, *Her Furnace*, etc). In Well, the steel curves out from the wall, as the steel cradles curve upwards from the floor in the floor pieces. Any number of affinities could be suggested for this motif of the cradle curving around the globe: the broad cuffs of 17th century costume enclosing a hand; the ruffs or frills of Elizabethan and Tudor times framing a head; an umbrella or parasol around a head; flower petals extending around the stamens and seeds.

Alison Wilding's use of meteoritic material (the tektites) automatically gives the pieces a cosmic and cosmological dimension (even though Wilding plays down such starry connotations, and does not refer to the origin of these chunks of material). Wilding admits to being fascinated by meteorites. 'I find the whole galaxy difficult to comprehend' she says (Wilding, 1991, 63). Wilding is as awed by outer space as even fully paid up astronomers who know how it all works (or think they do). If you think about it for even a moment, the universe is a really astonishing thing. Wilding explores some this strangeness with her tektite sculptures. Meteorites are rare – and expensive – you can buy little fragments of tektite, but not large pieces. Meteorites chime alchemically: like the Philosopher's Stone, they are distinctly other-worldly, made of a material not of this Earth. Meteorites are quite different from most other materials, being formed from the inter-planetary media of the universe. Indeed, in one sense, meteoritic material is rarer than gold. One of Wilding's most intriguing sculptures is a real iron meteorite mounted in plexiglass and set up high in a slanted window. The meteorite is framed against the sky. Clouds are seen moving behind it. It looks as if it's fallen and landed on the gallery window.[1]

Wilding then made a replica of the meteorite so it could be seen up close, instead of looking like a dark blob high up, distant from the viewer. Wilding's solution to the problem of displaying the replica meteorite (cast in bronze) was to encase it is resin, and have the resin shaped like...a potato. A number of images began to fuse: the tiny round meteorite travels through black space, like the potato growing in the equally black earth. Both meteorites and potatoes suggest seeds in blackness, and growth. They are both images of cells and seeds, images of things that start small land grow.

> The meteorite comes from darkness through to light. When the idea was suggested that it could be set in resin then I suddenly saw the way they could be, the way they are now. It's like a tadpole, like the birth of something but also the

end of something; or it's also exposure and immersion all in one place. (Wilding, 1991, 64)

Although she might dissuade people from reading her work in 'cosmic' or 'religious' or 'symbolic' terms, it is clear that Wilding interprets her own work to herself in these terms. The talk of seeds, cells, birth and growth is automatically cosmic and religious. These discourses of religion and symbolism may not be apparent as one views the work in a gallery, but they are there, waiting to be uncovered. The meteorite sculpture is called *Infinities*, which enhances the cosmological subtext: from the birth and growth of cells to the birth and growth of stars, and galaxies. Just as the night sky is mass of tiny particles which are actually gigantic stars and galaxies, so Wilding's little meteorite in its resin case alludes to huge structures made from tiny components: plants, animals, humans, planets. When Wilding encloses the meteorite cast in resin she isolates it from the quotidian world and exaggerates it. Putting it in resin makes us look at the little meteorite cast in a new way. It's the same with the piece of moon rock brought back by one of the Apollo moon shots which is set in a little glass pyramid in the Natural History Museum in London.

In the large sculpture *Stain* (1991) we seem to be in the midst of an alchemical experiment. A large piece of woollen cloth is spread over the floor, perhaps to represent staining liquid. The cloth spreads out from a tall structure which stands in what looks like a large upturned tin bath. The anthropological reading of *Stain* might be that it depicts someone standing up in a bath and the liquid pours out from *underneath* the bath. Like a strange flood, the cloth seeps out from underneath the bath-like structure. The cloth spilling over a form in *Stain* appears in an earlier work, *In the Brass* (1987). In *Plunder*, Irish linen is packed into a walnut container. It is the opposite of *Stain* and *Into the Brass*, where the cloth flows freely. While many works suggest liquid and the qualities of liquids (movement, transparency, viscosity), Wilding has not yet used liquids in her work. There are materials such as beeswax, and lead, which appear as semi-viscous elements. Wilding does not move into kinetic sculpture, though, like, say, Rebecca Horn with her rivers of bubbling, dripping mercury.

The cloth in *Into the Brass* and *Stain* both conceals and reveals. It functions like so many objects in Alison Wilding's sculpture, doing two seemingly contrary actions simultaneously. In *Into the Brass*, although the brass bowl is covered with the dark wool/ cotton cloth, the cloth itself is pierced with holes, so the brass can be seen underneath. Cloth covering an object in this way can be interpreted in a number of ways. People put cloths on furniture, to keep off dust. No, that's not it. People put covers on objects to hide them. That's closer. Cloths are thrown over statues or plaques before they are unveiled. Cloths also hide magical tricks and are thrown off at the end of the trick. But although the dark cloths of *Stain* and *Into the Brass* seem to concealing and keeping something secret, they also very clearly define the shape and volume of the metal structures underneath. The cloths define some of the sculptural forms with a sensual clarity. Further, the cloths have a distinctly liquid component. They spill over the floor, just like water (or blood perhaps?). In *Into the Brass*, there is an impression of the bowl overflowing with liquid, which spills over on all sides. It is an image of abundance and fecundity. In *Stain*, the cloth extends much further beyond the central steel structures than in Into the Brass. The cloth in both *Into the Brass* and *Stain* serves to define the field of the sculpture. One cannot go close to the central components, one cannot step on the cloth. They cloths thus cast a magnetic field around the sculptures, which simultaneously repels and attracts. And, like magnetic fields, the cloths echo the shapes of the metal forms at the centre.

It is not merely the sight of Wilding's sculptures which enable us to make the connection with mediæval alchemy. One could say of many artists' work that their forms echo those of alchemy. No, it is the sense of transformation in Wilding's work that makes her art alchemical. Wilding shows the transformation in operation. Her sculptures create a dynamic between two forms. The tension is produced by having one form large, the other small; or one made of stone, the other in metal; or one curving around another. The Postminimal sculpture *Displace*, shows the displacement of space in frozen time, with each of the three stages of the white plastic forms moving outwards from the black steel tower diminishing in size. They are like the echoes of the tower, dissipating into the area around the sculpture.

A sculpture such as *Fruit* suggests organic connotations in its title, and is a mass of brass rods which curl in and around a central lump of tektite. The material, tektite, is perhaps of meteoric origin. The web of brass rods suggests many kinds of organic forms, from veins and arteries in the body, to the movement and orbits of sub-atomic particles. If *Fruit* was by Rebecca Horn, there would be mercury, perhaps, flowing along the tangle of tubes. *Fruit* is already a dynamic work without being kinetic in the Rebecca Horn manner.

Alison Wilding's *Nature: Blue and Gold* is wonderful, and rich in the contrasts it throws up: between the soft wood and the hard gold, between the dull surface of the wood and the gleaming surface of the gold, between the carved wood and the constructed gold, between the thin plane of the gold and the rounded volume of the wood, between the pliant wood and the inflexible metal, between the patterned gold and the unpatterned wood, and so on.

ALISON WILDING AND CONSTANTIN BRANCUSI

Alison Wilding's sculptures are marked by a sense of light and dark, which Brancusi also celebrated. 'Brancusi seeks to distil a pure luminous essence,' writes Lynne Cooke, 'whereas Wilding celebrates the power of darkness.' (Cooke, 12) Cooke sees a further link between Alison Wilding and Brancusi: the sense of space around a sculpture, which Brancusi made clear by his use of pedestals. 'She abandons his base or pseudo-pedestal in favour of establishing a precinct or zone for the sculpture by means of the interaction of its components as well as by suggesting a deceptively fragile equilibrium.' (13)

Wilding's *Pond* is beautiful: a circular piece of copper, cut into zigzags upon which rest a small circle of slate, and a moon-shaped piece of Portland stone. This latter recalls one of Brancusi's *Fish* The sheet of copper representing the pond is not fixed together, thus, writes Lynne Cooke, reinforcing

> the feeling of delicacy so that this horizontal plane comes to resemble a meniscus, a taut but fragile surface on which far heavier objects can miraculously float.[2]

'I like *stuff* and not particular materials' Wilding says.[3] One can see how Wilding begins with materials, or rather, with 'stuff'. Intrigued by organic relationships between things, Wilding is naturally going to be interested in 'stuff' itself rather than material – that is, the stuff of life, life-stuff. Wilding also treats each material she works with in a similar manner. That is, no particular medium is used to the exclusion of others. She moves from beeswax to lime to wood to plastic to stone easily. There is no one particular medium which is her own, or which we associate with Wilding's sculpture. Works like *Bare* use 'man-made' or 'man-manipulated' materials, the metals – brass and copper, the materials, like stone, oil and marble,

47

which are regarded with suspicion by some feminist artists (King, op. cit.); while *Into the Dark*, with its limewood, lead and pigments, seems 'natural'. A work like *Inland* (1990) seems wholly postwar/ Post-minimal: it's a polypropylene sculpture, a series of tiers or strata, which looks 'uncharacteristic'.[4] The use of such plastics inevitably has connotations with Minimal sculpture and sculptors such as Eva Hesse. *Inland* is the Wilding sculpture most like a Minimal sculpture (it's like Donald Judd's 'ladders' or wall sculptures). Wilding spoke of desiring an effect of exposure, where what you see is what you get: 'I wanted the skin of the work, its surface, to be its mass and density.'[5] A work such as *Fugue* (1992) also uses polypropylene, but, as is typical in Wilding's art, the material does not appear artificial.

In 1991 at Dean Clough (Halifax) Wilding created a site specific sculpture, *Pulse*, for the Henry Moore Sculpture Trust. *Pulse* was a large walk through sculpture of white polypropylene, more an installation than a 'sculpture'. Wilding had produced installations before 1991 – much of her work in the 70s, after she had left the Royal College, was installation work (Wilding, 1991, 62). In Halifax there was an opportunity to go to town on a gallery space. Developing her sculpture in the space at Dean Clough created many logistic and æsthetic challenges, and at times Wilding found she was losing overall control of the work. The two spaces were light and dark, and Wilding responded directly to the sense of illumination. *Pulse* is thus a light work, which explores the relation to light, while sculptures such as *Assembly* and *Stain* deal with darkness. *Pulse* was the result of many compromises, and Wilding was adamant that the staircase piece would stick to her original conception. In the end, she had to change many aspects of it, which proved disheartening. *Pulse* was intended to be about entering a different kind of interiority, separate from the surrounding gallery space, but also complementing it. Like so many of Wilding's sculptures, it was meant to isolate a space of its own while at the same time reacting to the space around itself. Wilding was also conscious of trying to manipulate the viewer's sense of space, so that one moved through a series of different spaces. There was a movement from familiar spaces to unfamiliar ones, from spaces that were 'conventional' to spaces that disrupted convention. At Dean Clough, Wilding aimed to provide a different sense of time, space and matter from the usual gallery or museum experience. Of her Halifax work she said:

> I think the whole space encourages people to stay a long time. It's partly to do with the location, since many people travel quite a long way to go there and so probably want to spend a long time, and maybe want to go out and come back and really make sense of it. I think the place is geared to the art, not to a kind of consumerism. (Wilding, ib., 64)

The large walk through sculpture *Pulse* and the tiny meteorite were seen as symbiotic structures, even though one was very large and one very small. To emphasize the sense of interiority, Wilding had the windows of the gallery varnished over and stippled with sponges. She explored similar notions of opacity in works such as *Veiled no 2* in Cornwall. As a structure, with its hard white edges and large planes of plastic, *Pulse* owes much to the Minimalists, to artists such as Donald Judd and Robert Morris. Another Postminimal work, *Seal*, contains a white polypropylene form, something like a cube, recalling the rigorous mathematical cubes of Sol LeWitt. The severity of *Seal*'s near-cube is modulated by the presence right next to it of a sandstone block, deliberately roughly carved. Though much smaller than the white plastic structure, the stone block turns out to be much more assertive, much more intriguing as a form.

WILDING'S SCULPTURE AS GODDESS ART

Deep (1984) is a tall sheet of metal curved around and standing over a smallish 'nodule', an egg-shaped volume. There is a slit or hole cut in the sheet, just above the egg-shape, again suggesting all manner of organic allusions – to the interpenetration of organic forms, where one relies on the other for its existence. In *Curvature* (1985), another egg-shaped form stands slightly apart from a curved sheet of metal, which again has a notch cut in it. There are any number of readings one could make of this sort of sculpture: the sheet of metal, for instance, could be 'protecting' the small egg-shape, keeping it shielded, though from what, who can say. Mary Rose Beaumont sees Wilding's *Hearth* (1986), which she describes as 'a single hollow monolith', as an equivalent of Piero della Francesca's *Madonna del Parto* (Beaumont, 79). Piero's Madonna at Monterchi causes controversy. The people of Monterchi do not like it being moved. The local women regard the picture of the pregnant Madonna as holy. When the painting was going to be moved in 1954 to Florence for an exhibition, the Mayor of Monterchi 'dared not risk lending it...fearing possible reactions if, during the absence, a woman had a miscarriage.'[6]

Like the abstractions of Alison Wilding's sculptures, the Madonna in Piero's painting is simultaneously other-worldly and so definitely *there*. Piero's pregnant Madonna is the most powerful example of this type of painting.[7] The *Madonna del Parto* exudes a similar magnificence to the *Madonna della Misericordia*. There is the same total authority and self-confidence in her stance, the same symmetry, the same dominant figure flanked by assistants. Wilding's floor-standing sculptures have some of this 'monumental' grandeur. Like Brancusi's *Birds in Space*, Wilding's *Curvature* and *Deep* exude an authority, a self-confidence, a self-contained form of presence, much like the parthenogenic Goddess in Piero's *Madonna del Parto*. For Piero's Birthing Madonna needs no male deity to quicken her into life: she is parthenogenic, a self-fulfilling being.

Belly forward, with her hand on her womb, the Madonna is caught in an archetypal stance of a pregnant woman. Piero's *Birthing Madonna* is quite clearly an image of the Black Goddess, the Goddess as fertile Mother, the deity who 'presides especially over marriage and sex, pregnancy and childbirth'.[8] Piero's Goddess openly displays her sexuality: the *Madonna and Child* paintings of the Renaissance displace and decentre sexuality, repressing and suppressing it. But the pregnant Madonna in *Madonna del Parto* is distinctly sexual. The swollen belly is unmistakable. The *Madonna del Parto* is one of the most famous of magical paintings. Seemingly humble, Piero's *Childbirthing Madonna* presides over the whole matrifocal experience of motherhood, birth and life. Piero's *Madonna del Parto* looks like a pre-Christian deity, a *diva* or *prima donna*, an austere Goddess dressed in a simply-cut blue dress. With a similar austerity, Wilding's sculpture has simple shapes and patterns, those cylinders with slits or arches cut in them, or bowls of hemlock on Brancusi-like pedestals.

Some of Wilding's cone or column-like sculptures refer directly to religion in their titles: *Vestal*, for instance. Works such as *Immersion, Receiver, Nest, Her Furnace, Vestal, Tidal, Bare, Fugue* and *Dismantle* all feature cylindrical forms, most of them floor-standing. Some of these forms recall monumental figures, others suggest notions of cradling and protection. Some of the slender standing sculptures have openings at the top, inviting the viewer to peer down into their interiors – Vestal, Immersion, Her Furnace. The act of looking down into the sculpture becomes an important part of consuming the work. The identification with the interior institutes a new sense of self-awareness, a new sense of the body.[9]

One of the most common of Wilding's motifs is one form nestling inside another. Sometimes the two forms fit snugly together, as in *Nest*, while others, such as *Immersion* and *Temper,* have more of a gap between the upper, narrow form and the lower, wider form. Immersion unites two of Wilding's favourite forms, the gently tapering upright cylinder and the shallow cone. The notion of 'immersion' is suggested here in two ways: firstly, as with *Nest*, the upper form is 'immersed' in the lower form, just as a limb is lowered into water. But, secondly, the notions of inner and outer are emphasized by Wilding's treatment of the surface of this all-brass sculpture. The inner surfaces gleam, as brass gleams around hearths in pre-industrial age houses or in ye olde pubs. The exterior surface of the brass, the skin of the sculpture, is not polished, but darkened.

Bare (1989-90) has an inside/outside, immersion/ exposure theme like *Immersion*. It is an upright floor-standing work in two of Wilding's favourite metals, copper and brass. Out of the tapering brass cylinder copper braid arms extend, much like limbs of the branches of a tree or plant. The organic discourse of *Bare* is emphasized by the holes lower down the sculpture, as if the copper cables or branches had been cut off, or withered and fell off, or, just as likely, are waiting to grow. Other details of *Bare* entice: the notch cut in the top of the brass column, and the tangled interior into which one can peer. The interior of *Bare* is a web of copper tubes – just as, just under the skin, there are hundreds of interconnecting veins and tubes. These are the hidden mechanisms of organic life, which sustain it.

In *Tidal* (1990-1) the metaphor/ analogy of 'immersion and exposure' suggests one of the most fundamental and poetic forms of diastolic motion. The tides move in and out, ceaselessly, every day and every day since time immemorial, over millions of years. This natural rhythm of water flooding in and out, high then low, is so basic to life it's taken for granted. One imagines the sea and tides will appear more in Wilding's work in the 90s after her time in Cornwall, living near the sea. The ocean envelops places such as St Ives and the Lizard – one is always glimpsing it, behind houses, along alleys, beyond gardens. At St Ives, the Porthmeor art studios back onto the beach, so that one has the sea as a permanent presence outside the window. On the tablelands of the Lizard and the central ridge of moorland of West Penwith one sees the sea on three sides. In summer it's an incandescent azure presence; in winter, a grey smudge. The harsh rocky landscape is the closest Britain gets to Greece and the Mediterranean – the archaic, uncompromising Greece of the ancient, mythic world. There is distinctly something about Cornwall that attracts poets, painters, sculptors and artists. It's to do with many factors, but landscape, the sea, the light, the isolation, the Celtic undercurrent, the weather and the wildness, must have something to do with it.

The tide immerses long sections of the landscape under water then exposes them again. This rhythm of immersion/ exposure is invoked in Wilding's *Tidal.* A giant brass cylinder rises out of a large hollow triangular tube. One form is tall and stands upright; the other is horizontal, lying down. The triangular tube suggests the Earth, something solid under the brass column. The symbolism of the triangle is also of water, and the feminine (the triangle is a symbol of female genitals, etc). Tidal motion is primarily a rising and falling of water levels, and this is what Wilding's *Tidal* suggests. Beside rivers and harbours there are poles with scales painted on them to measure the rise and fall of floods and tides. The brass column in *Tidal* recalls those measuring sticks.

4

Relationships of Nurturance

The moment we start to talk about the *meaning* of Wilding's work, we move into the realm of pure conjecture.[1] We know we respond to her work, but to exactly what it is in her work that excites us, it's very difficult to say. It is something to do with organic forms, with relations between the various parts of the sculpture,[2] something to do with the materials, which are acutely sensuous (wax, wood, gold, brass, oil).

There is something animal-like and organic about Wilding's rounded, egg-shaped forms, as in *Indelible Field*, where two narrow strips of metal enclose a wooden egg-shape in the centre. The strips form an enclosure around the central volume, with curves suggestive of organic forms. It's not perhaps surprising that the egg form should appear so often in Wilding's work. It is a form that is malleable, physically as well as symbolically. It is a form that serves sculptors well, merging into the globe on the one hand, and the irregular 'potato' or 'boulder' shape on the other. The egg form suggests the outer organic forms, such as seeds, heads, eyes, stones, as well as 'inner' or hidden forms, such as internal organs, wombs, and the basic building blocks of animal life, cells. Often Wilding's egg shapes are made from wood, such as the holed egg in *Receiver* which nestles up to the severe looking steel cone. Wilding has treated the surface of the oak egg she's carved: she's rubbed beeswax and pigment into it, darkening it, and ageing the surface, so it looks like a huge nut, or a vast seed pod. In *Fruit* the egg form has exploded, sending out a web of shoots like a seed, frantically growing back in on itself. Another oak sculpture, *Beneath the Skin* (1986) has the same stippled, rubbed surface texture. As it's a wall sculpture, the underside is an important feature, and the height above the floor becomes crucial. The sculptor controls how much of the underside the viewer is permitted to see simply by placing the work high or low. The wall piece *Possession* shows the inside of the egg shape. Again made from treated oakwood, *Possession* encloses a small form in the centre. As with *Blue Skies*, it suggests a small form being nurtured by a large form, perhaps an embryo in the womb.

Easy to spot the notions of motherhood, of one form enfolding and nurturing another, in Alison Wilding's works. In these abstract sculptures, one can move in any direction, in terms of connotations and readings. But it is clearly the *relationship* between two elements, that really fascinates Wilding. Always we find one material set against another, or one in conjunction with another, touching another. 'Set against' is the wrong term, for clearly Wilding's twin forms are in a relationship that is not necessarily antagonistic: one thinks of empathy, or tenderness even, in Wilding's works. Greg Hilty writes:

> duality, or double significance, is typical of Alison Wilding's work, which most often consists of two distinct shapes, and two contrasting materials, set in balance or in dynamic tension with each other.[3]

Often one element is large, the other, small.[4] The two elements are usually luscious and mysterious, at once semi-figurative and beyond interpretation, though some interpret them as masculine and feminine elements,[5] the twin poles of heterosexuality, which are involved in some arcane dance or dalliance.[6] The elements in Wilding's sculptures are odd couples, not even pairs. They are not like two playing cards – the same object but with a slightly different appearance: the ace of hearts and two of diamonds, say. Wilding's pairs of objects are more like a pear and a stick of wood, or a granite boulder and a patch of grass. They are related (both pear and stick come from a tree) but with different characteristics. Each object in the Wildingian pair bond (in *Stormy Weather, Dismantle, Brim, Receiver*) has a different function from the other. Each object looks different, has different qualities of texture, reflectivity, weight, size and shape. 'Different' in so many ways, they are also together, they are also in intimate relationship with each other. One cannot exist without the other without radically changing either one. The partnership may be unwilling or angst-ridden, tender or empathic, but it is a partnership nevertheless.

The dualistic nature of Wilding's work is emphasized by the artist herself, who speaks of a work being one thing but also its opposite. Thus, of Pulse, she says it is

> about 'immersion' as well as about 'exposure'. I don't think you can have one without the other. (Wilding, 1991, 65)

Perhaps the chief characteristic of dualist systems is that both elements are essential, and one cannot survive without the other. In the West, there is good/ evil, God/ Devil, right/ wrong, Earth/ Heaven, Heaven/ Hell, light/ dark, day/ night, male/ female, etc, and in the Orient terms such as *yin/ yang, shiva/ shakti.* Yet one of the other characteristics of dualistic systems is the urge towards unity and union, towards the reconciliation of opposites. This is an underlying goal in Christian mysticism, and in philosophies such as alchemy, Taoism and Tantrism. Behind the duality is the unity, and one might see in Wilding's work a striving towards unity. True, most of her sculptures look like they are locked in the struggle of becoming, of travelling not arriving, of always being dual never unified. But even being in the same partnership is a kind of unity, and although sculptures such as *Brim, Fuse* and *Stormy Weather* look like they'll never finally 'fuse' or be unified, they are themselves unified in their working together.

As objects to be viewed and consumed, Wilding's sculptures do not offer a single viewpoint, but many. There is not one 'preferred' way of viewing the sculpture, not this side of from that angle. Rather, Wilding prefers a circularity of viewpoints, viewing many sides. In *Untitled* (1980), a floor piece, a narrow strip of metal forms an enclosure in the midst of which is a metal structure consisting of two slabs of metal leaning against each other. The strip does not make an exact circle, but even so marks out a space separate from the rest of the gallery. It is an oval boundary, beyond which the spectator is not permitted to step. The 1991 sculpture *Assembly* deals with notions of inside and outside, immersion and exposure: a large PVC network of strips stands in front of a steel cover. The orange-hued plastic fits inside the steel shell. The one structure is perhaps intended to 'protect' the other.

The 1994 piece *Meridian II* is two thin strips of metal joined together at the centre with a large chunk of polyester resin. It is a wall sculpture: the spikes of metal, one brass and one copper, extend outwards, like two wings. Another 1994 sculpture, Pair I, is two smallish metal structures – hollow tubes with a lip-like shape at the top. Like *Vestal*, these are narrow, tall sculptures, that gradually expand in size towards the top. The flared openings at the top recall flowers – the lily, for instance. It's easy to anthropomorphize these two free standing sculptures on their wooden display stand. They do *look* like two figures, but Wilding's sculpture is not as easily interpreted as that. There is a type of classical music called 'programme' music, music which has a definite 'theme' or subject. But some composers (and critics) loathe it when some sort of simplistic imagery is attached to music, so that the music can only illustrate that particular scene. Similarly, Wilding's sculptures will not rest with a single interpretation, there isn't a single reading 'programmed' into her abstract but semi-organic forms. A sculpture such as *Scree* (1984) seems to be 'literal'. A partial cone of brass is fixed to a wall. It is small – less than foot in each dimension. In the cone is some sand. Because the cone of *Scree* is on its side the sand slides down, it seems to look like a rock scree, it seems to refer to a real natural feature in the world. But wait a minute, the sand is tinted *blue*. It looks more like water than rock. Again, as so often with Alison Wilding's work, the sculpture's allusiveness is only one aspect of it. The poetry of the form itself, the blue-hued sand sliding down the metal cone sticking out of the wall, takes over. As Hepworth says, '[w]orking in the abstract way seems to release one's personality and sharpen the perceptions so that in the observation of humanity or landscape it is the wholeness of inner intention which moves one so profoundly.' (Witzling, 286)

Stormy Weather and a sculpture related to it, *Fuse*, are dualistic pieces, founded on the Wildingian notions of relationship and union. The title *Stormy Weather* is of course distinctly programmatic and allusive. Yes, one can read the evocation of or allusion to a storm in *Stormy Weather*. The primary motif of the sculpture, however, is relationship and duality. The two structures which make up *Stormy Weather* are not a pair, not evenly matched. Like so many of Wilding's dual sculptures, these two objects are definitely an 'odd couple'. Although we might strive to transcend metaphor, we can't help anthropomorphizing sculptures even when using the cool, formal terms of art criticism. Thus, the steel structure in *Stormy Weather* does indeed seem to be 'leaning' towards the taller bronze structure. There's always a problem in using anthropomorphic equivalents, turning the inanimate objects into living being which 'lean' towards each other, which 'protect' each other. *Stormy Weather* doesn't move, as an animal moves, but it is, like many of Wilding's sculptures, dynamic, creating, like Brancusi's *Birds in Space*, a movement in stillness, a suggestion of movement. Back to metaphor, then, back to *suggestions, hints, allusions, equivalents* of this or that.

Fuse (1990) seems to have completed the union of two elements, this time leaded steel and plastic. Even without the aid of the title, Fuse is clearly about some kind of union. The two structures are enclosed together. In the anthropomorphic view, they are two figures in a new kind of harmony: they present edges which nearly fuse together. In the romantic sense, they might lovers, like in Brancusi's *The Kiss*, where the lovers sit eye to eye, lip to lip, head to head, breast to breast, bodies flush against each other. In Brancusi's *The Kiss* not a slither of air is allowed to separate the mystical union: in Wilding's *Fuse*, there is a slender curving gap between the steel and the plastic structures. The union is not total, and Wilding emphasizes the differences between the two objects: the polypropylene is black and the steel is light grey; the steel object has a rounded back, while the polypropylene is pointed. *Hearth*, (1986), a single standing structure, is constructed out of two curved halves of thin metal. The two sections are joined together at the top by a narrow loop of metal. Though they seem separate, the two forms curve towards each other, creating gently enclosed space, which's more open at the top.

Wilding's twin forms have affinities with the double stars of astronomy, as found in the Plough or Great Bear: one stars orbits around the other: it is a mutual orbit. One thinks of the brother and sister or King and Queen of alchemy, which fuse to form the hermaphrodite, the Divine Being, the One, the Philosopher's Stone. Other erotic and spiritual dualities include, in British folklore, the May King and May Queen, the Green Man and his bride, and the gnostic *syzygy*, which is two souls 'yoked' together, that is, two spirits forming a Platonic whole, like two yokes in one egg. Two yokes in an egg is a metaphor that would surely appeal to a sculptor, especially one such as Wilding or Brancusi.

The erotic dimension of Wilding's sculpture recalls the gender dualities of alchemical forms. It is the *relationships* between the elements in alchemy (among other things) that is important: alchemy celebrates the union between silver and gold, for instance, or between sulphur and mercury, often symbolized by the celestial conjunction of the sun and the moon, or day and night, or Venus and Mars, the Queen and King of symbolism. In alchemical treatises, the unification of the 'Great Work', as it's called, is symbolized mainly in two ways: by a man and woman copulating, and by a hermaphrodite. Wilding's sculptures, such as *Stormy Weather, Blue Skies* and *Vestal* suggest forms in a symbolic, interdependent relationship.

In alchemy, the hermaphrodite is created in vessels, as depicted in those haunting treatises, such as Mylis' *Philosophia reformata* (of 1622) or the *Rosarium Philosophorum* series (of 1550). Alchemy presents an impossibility: a living human being who is simultaneously male and female. The hermaphrodite stands proudly on the ground, legs apart, displaying male and female genitals, the vulva next to the penis.[7] In some alchemical treatises the king and queen make love on a tomb: Wilding's sculptures do not partake of such obvious patriarchal ideologies. Sex and death are eternally conjoined in masculinist ideology. Stressing the alchemical nature of Alison Wilding's sculpture, we must remember that she creates in a contemporary, feminist era. Though no 'feminist' herself, in the radical sense of the term (as applied to Andrea Dworkin, Catherine MacKinnon, Hélène Cixous and Susan Griffin), Wilding does take on board feminist notions. Thus, while emphasizing the exploration of gender in Wilding's work and comparing it with the evocation of masculinity and femininity in mediæval alchemy, we must also keep in mind that Wilding's sculptures always retain a sense of ambiguity. Wilding's work cultivates an ambivalent sense of

61

gender and eroticism. There is no definite 'goal' in her work, in the sense that there is in alchemy, or in 'malestream' artists such as Picasso, Klimt, Rodin and Henry Moore. Alison Wilding explores an area of art where gender blurs into mystery, where relationships remain unfixed and fluid, where the one certainty is that there is no certainty of interpretation. Self-consciously cultivating a sense of mystery and ambiguity can backfire: it has backfired for many artists. They are called pretentious. Wilding's sculpture, though, manages to remain mysterious and ambiguous without looking pretentious or shallow. Wilding's work does not strain for effects: rather, it achieves them seemingly effortlessly. Like other great art, Wilding's sculptures have an immediate sense of presence. They are *there*, and they look as if they've always been there. They have that 'obviousness' that some art has: as if it has always been around. When you hear a 'classic' or 'great' work of music – Bach's B-minor Requiem, for instance, or The Beatles' *Sgt Pepper*, it's as if the work has always been around. It seems so obvious and so right, you wonder how no one has made it before. Even 'ancient' works, like the Pyramids in Egypt, seem so obvious it's a wonder people didn't make them ten thousand years earlier. (Perhaps they didn't want to – that's another matter). Alison Wilding's *Hemlock III, Stormy Weather* and *Immersion* seem so *right*, like Brancusi's *Birds in Space* or Paul Klee's *Fish Magic*.

Wilding's dual elements revolve around each other, moving into each other, in a dance of alchemical transmutation. One element of Wilding's art on its own may be delicious and full of presence, but in conjunction with another element, all sorts of tensions are set up. Hilary Gresty writes:

> Alison Wilding's work throughout her career and in innumerable ways, has tested the relationship between the self and the rest of the world. Edges, boundaries, the relationship of one thing to another, the visible and the concealed, the intimate and the public, the contained and the unimagined, ambiguity, balance and rhythm are some of the elements of her sculptural language. (*Bare*, 8)

The relation between the two elements in Wilding's work is not always 'equal', either. Often one form is much smaller than the other. Or one is softly rounded, while the other is jagged and hard. Or one is of a 'soft' material, like wood, and the other is a hard material, like steel. In *Hard for Hard* (1984), a boat-like shape, of metal, rests one of its ends on an egg-shape. Here the relationship is of supporting and being supported: the one leans on the other, just as people 'lean' on each other, psychologically and socially as well as physically.

In Wilding's sculpture, the forms are not static, they are in motion. A sense of change is highlighted, as in land art. The sense of mystery is cultivated, so that ambiguity is the norm. What Jean Fisher writes of the artist Avis Newman could also apply to Alison Wilding:

> The work's space is one of fluidity, of swells and eddies, in which contours and volumes - now transparent, now opaque - gently turn and undulate in a movement that is both sinuous and sensuous.[8]

Wilding's art can be seen as employing some of the strategies of feminist art, then: Wilding's work uses openness, a 'non-hierarchical' use of materials, and a language of multiplicity which disturbs notions dear to patriarchy (linearity, rationality, exact categorization/ classification, etc). Wilding's work refuses to be fixed to a single meaning or reading. This is not a product of indecision or inadequacy, but a refusal to have everything subsume to one meaning.

Discussing the painter Therese Oulton, a contemporary of Alison Wilding, Rosa Lee, in "Resisting amnesia: feminism, painting and postmodernism", said that Oulton's work allowed for a release from the dominance of 'any one fixed interpretation'.[9] Therese Oulton's abstract paintings, like Wilding's sculptures, refuse an all-encompassing interpretation or æsthetic. For Peter Gidal, Oulton's paintings 'disavow any stable female identity'.[10] I n discussing women's abstract work, whether painting or sculpture, one can see (usually masculinist) critics finding the non-representations difficult, even threatening. While critics can look at Rothko, Pollock, Newman and other Abstract Expressionist artists as purveying an art of full of 'tragic' feelings (Rothko), existential uncertainty and alienation (Pollock) or sublime heroism (Newman), with *female* abstract artists, nothing is as certain. Wilding's work, like Oulton's, straddles High Modernism and postmodernism, it moves between masculinist and feminist notions of 'art', it refuses description while hinting at full-blown lyricism, it seems feminist, 'pre-oedipal', pre-Symbolic, pre-masculinist, it shifts parameters which masculinist criticism cannot fully grasp and wield.

Wilding's wall-piece *Green Beak* is typical: two materials, slate and copper, are set together, the patinated copper extending below the smaller chunk of slate. Again, organic connotations abound, not only because of the title. Thus, it's easy to see the hanging down piece as a 'tongue' or a 'beak'. Orbit II (1994) is a small hemi-sphere displayed on a wall at eye level, or just above eye level, depending on how tall the viewer is (in art criticism, the viewer is usually assumed to be male – a white, First World, bourgeois male, average height 5 foot 10, say). *Orbit II*, made from brass and copper, looks like a hat or a skull cap. The half sphere has little holes in it. *Crown I*, another tall sculpture, is mounted much higher than eye level. Like Orbit II, it is a small sculpture, quite self-contained.

Titles in Wilding's sculpture, though, are really a form of 'working titles'. That is, the titles are only vaguely descriptive of the work: *Blueblack*, for instance, or *Nature: Blue and Gold*. Wilding's titles are like those of the abstract painter Agnes Martin, merely signposts towards something far deeper in the work. Some titles speak of water, cycles, nature movements of exposure and immersion: *Tidal, Inland, Exposure, Immersion, Infinities*, some speak of duality and union: *Fuse, Possession*, and its opposite, disharmony and separation: *Displace*. Some sculptures have vessel or nurturing titles: *Well, Nest, Fuse, Hearth, Receiver*. Some speak of moving into and under something: *Into the Dark, Into the Brass, Immersion, Beneath the Skin*. A title like *Green Beak* suggests one or two interpretations; it narrows down the interpretations of the sculpture, but it does not, like any title, limit them. For, as Barthes says, a work or text can have any number of meanings. Wilding's titles, then, offer only the vaguest, most ambiguous guides to her art. With sculpture, as with painting, we are always drawn to the object itself. The title is to be quickly forgotten (unless, as in the 60s Conceptual work of Lawrence Weiner or Bruce Nauman, the title is the work of art).

5

The Sculpture of Embrace:
Eroticism in Alison Wilding's Work

Alison Wilding directly embraces the potential for sculpture to be supremely sensual. Her abstract forms suggest intimate experiences, investigations of sexuality and the relations between space, imagination, fantasy and the body. The title of the sculpture *Into the Dark* suggests a movement into mystery, into the Night, which is the realm of the Goddess and feminine mysteries. With titles such as *Into the Dark* and *Deep*, Wilding evokes a world beneath the visible one, a world of darkness and mystery, a realm of invisible but powerful feelings. *Into the Dark* is a limewood form something like a horse's saddle or a bust without the head. In a distinctly vulvic shape is lead. As with *Minge* and other sculptures, Wilding, like Judy Chicago and Mary Beth Edelson, creates vulva images.

Sexuality in Wilding is immediately apparent, as in her sculpture *Minge* (1982). This is made from a left-over piece of metal, looking distinctly bird-like, with two pointed 'wings'. In the centre, though, the sensuality of the sculpture is made apparent by a red triangle made with a wax crayon heated up. 'There is exuberance in the way it makes wings of legs, like a sexual cherub' wrote John McEwen (57). Wings extending out from some core, globe or cylinder is a favourite Wilding motif. Sculptures such as *Meridian II* and *Hemlock II* feature little wings either side of a central node. The sexual connotations are both obvious and limiting: the wings as labia and the nodule as a clitoris is an obvious parallel, and, in the case of *Minge*, it is deliberately meant. It is limiting, too, for Wilding's sculpture, like any sculpture, goes far beyond a genital or body-centred sensuality. The eroticism of Wilding's sculpture, like most sculpture, is not confined to vulvas, clitorises or penises; neither is it limited to any particular part of the body, or any particular sexual or gender identity; or any particular sort of sexuality; or any particular socio-political interpretatiion of sexuality. Thus, the work and title, *Minge*, like Wilding's other sculptures, is not feminist nor anti-feminist, not for this or that form of sexuality or sexual politics, not wholly representational nor wholly abstract.

Wilding's *Hemlock III* is, like her *Blueblack*, a wooden dish containing hemlock, lead, and beeswax, hinting at alchemical transmutations. The dish with its dangerous substances is a kind of womb, a motif or experience that appears in much of modern sculpture, from Judy Chicago's *Dinner Table* to the womb interiors of Louise Bourgeoise and others. *Blueblack* is another dish set up on a softly rounded pedestal. The dish extends into space to one side, away from the centre of gravity of the support. In Blueblack the dish contains lead, a variant on *Hemlock III*. One wonders what is being offered here, and why: the lead and hemlock in *Blueblack* and *Hemlock III* is being lifted forwards and upwards to the spectator, as if enticing them to partake of their poisonous material. Blueblack and *Hemlock III* are displaying their dangerous substances, not hiding them. There is no secret interior here as in *Immersion* or *Vestal*. The lead and hemlock is there for all to see.

Wilding herself stresses the enigmatic nature of her work: '[t]he obverse of making is looking, not telling',[1] and she emphasizes, as so many artists do, the making of the sculpture: '[t]he making and doing processes [are] always the mainspring of the work'.[2] There is a point beyond which we cannot go, it seems: that is, we move, finally, into a realm of mystery, where we are not sure how we are meant to be reading Wilding's sculptures. Finally, Wilding's work *is* mysterious, but it does not self-consciously cultivate mystery, as, says, Claes Oldenburg or Jeff Koons or Andy Warhol or Yves Klein or Robert Rauschenberg self-consciously drew attention to the manufacture of art. Wilding is not a postmodernist in this sense: she cultivates a sense of the object, of the 'objecthood' of sculpture. So mystery remains.

Bare looks so much like a body: an upright cylinder immediately refers to the body, to that 'little body upright' as Samuel Beckett says in one of his short stories. *Bare* stands on the floor, with six curved 'arms', its cylinder trunk pitted with holes. Wilding's *Veiled No. 2*, made in 1993, is an object inside another object, something like a miniature obelisk inside an opaque cone. There are two cones in *Veiled No. 2*, inside one is a honey-coloured obelisk, inside the other, a black obelisk. The cones cover the obelisks, in that 'protecting' or 'nurturing' gesture we have mentioned before in Wilding's work. The works *Veiled No. 2* and *Exposure* are pieces made in or about Alison Wilding's time working in a studio in Cornwall. Wilding worked in a studio at Porthallow on the wonderful Lizard peninsula. Cornwall has been an important experience for Wilding. The significance of Cornwall is not expressed in obvious ways, but it is there. For instance, for her 1995 show at her dealers, Karsten Schubert in London, Wilding had a photograph she'd taken put on the private view announcement card of Goonhilly Earth Station, one of the famous landmarks of South West Cornwall, seen on every tourist brochure. The gigantic radio dishes look impressive and 'futuristic' in the wild heathland of the Lizard, and can be seen for miles around, silhouetted against the ever-changing Cornish sky. The Lizard, where Wilding has made some of her 90s work, is one of the most atmospheric parts of Britain. The flora and fauna of the Lizard is rightly celebrated, and the geology of the place – the green and red Serpentine rock, the hard granite, make it a great place for sculptor.[3] It is a place, too, that actually *makes* weather.

Cornwall is having yet another artistic renaissance with the opening of the Tate Gallery in St Ives in 1993. But long before the new Tate Gallery raised the cultural profile of Cornwall artists were making work in and around West Penwith. Before the Tate, there were lesser known attractions at St Ives, often hidden away, such as Bob Devereux's Salthouse Gallery, the Bernard Leach Pottery, the New Craftsman Gallery, the secluded Barbara Hepworth Museum and Sculpture Garden, the large Penwith Gallery, and the old studios around Porthmeor and Back Road West; in Penzance there's the Rainyday Gallery, and the wonderful Wolf at the Door gallery in Bread Street with its tiny but exquisite upstairs gallery; and then Newlyn Art Gallery, where Wilding had one of her major shows. Taken together, in one broad sweep, the number of talented artists who worked in St Ives or West Penwith at one time or another is quite extraordinary, considering the tiny scale of the place: Barbara Hepworth, Ben Nicholson, Patrick Heron, Francis Bacon, Bernard Leach, Naum Gabo, Alfred Wallis, Terry Frost, Peter Lanyon, Adrian Stokes, Wilhelmina Barns-Graham, David Bomberg, Alan Davie, Roger Hilton, Bryan Wynter and Breon O'Casey. The roll-call of distinguished visitors includes Mark Rothko, Victor Pasmore, Helen Frankenthaler, Mark Tobey, Larry Rivers and Laura Knight.

In Cornwall one cannot ignore the number of prehistoric sites, the menhirs, cairns, quoits, burial chambers, prehistoric huts and the stone circles. The places are instantly poetic: Boscawen-Ûn, Tregeseal and Merry Maidens stone circles; Carn Euny and Chysauster ancient settlements; the Mên-an-Tol holed stone; Lanyon, Zennor, Mulfra and Chun Quoits; the holy wells of Madron, Euny and Sancreed. Alison Wilding has spoken of prehistoric monuments and the relationship they have with the land. In her conversation with Michael Tooby she remarks on the way the ancient sites gradually reveal themselves as you climb up to them. She describes the slow ascent to a burial chamber, which makes the site and the surrounding landscape uncover themselves slowly (Wilding, 1994, 11) One can apply this sense of something being gradually revealed to Wilding's own work. One can see that her sculptures are not superficial objects which deliver up their meaning all at once, they are not objects of 'instant gratification'. It's not, though, that the spectator has to 'work' with the sculptures to get the best out of them. Rather, Wilding suggests a slow appraisal, rather a cursory glance. Not for Wilding's sculpture the millisecond glance most artworks receive from visitors to the big museums and galleries around the world.

At the Tate Gallery in St Ives, you find the two opaque cones of Veiled No. 2 perched high on a window sill at the head of the main stairwell in the gallery. It's an odd place for the sculpture, but the window sill location is explained by Wilding: it's up there because the general public handled the works too roughly. In the booklet that accompanies Wilding's Cornish stint, *Veiled No. 2* is photographed against the garden and the segment of the Lizard Wilding could see from her studio window. This siting is perfect, for Wilding's late sculptures, *Exposure, Seal* and *Veiled No. 2*, are very much concerned with notions of light and dark, transparency and opacity.

Alison Wilding's acute sensitivity to notions such as transparency and opacity is apparent from her statements. For example, she says: 'Complete transparency – seeing everything, can be quite shocking' (Wilding, 1991, 7). This is an odd thing to say – that transparency can be 'shocking'. But it fits in with the powerful emotions Wilding's work stir up. Seemingly quiet and passive on the surface, Wilding's work is in fact about primal experiences. The opacity in *Veiled No. 2*, for instance, is produced by rubbing pumice powder into the cones. This seemingly ordinary aspect of *Veiled*, the slightly opaque nature of the cones, is in fact the product of something everyone who lives by the sea is conscious of: the drift of salt spray. Wilding talks of the windows at her studio in Cornwall becoming 'opaque with salt spray after stormy weather.' (ib., 7) For those who live on coasts, salt spray is a part of everyday life. You taste it on your lips, your glasses get misted over with salt water.

Light is one Wilding's chief æsthetic concerns. Most of her sculptures explore the relation between the seen and the suggested, between the obvious and the hidden, the outer and the inner, between dullness and shininess. Many sculptures, for example, are semi-opaque (*Pulse, Fugue, Jar, Seal*), where one sees vaguely, never distinctly. Other sculptures are dark and matt and opaque on the outside, but shiny and luminous on the inside: *Immersion, Bare*, etc. As Richard Deacon writes of Wilding's

> obsessive concern for light...rubber penumbras, glint of brass or copper, blackened lumps of wood, misty steel sheets, perforated metal...

In Veiled, Wilding transforms the artificiality of clear plastic, making it 'naturalized' by rubbing it with pumice powder, to make the cones go misty. With *Exposure*, a much larger work, which is very much about the new Tate Gallery at St Ives, Wilding spoke of wanting to to let the sculpture age naturally. The notion of 'exposure' is both psychological and physical: *Exposure* is on the edge of the gallery, leaning out into space. Seeing the landscape through the sculpture is part of the experience of the sculpture. The black rubber coils offer a weighty, dark counterpoint to the lightness of the transparent plastic cone. The work at once is 'exposed' to the Cornish elements, and shelters in its niche in the roof of the Tate Gallery. For Wilding, the notion of 'exposure' is about being on display, either to the ravages of the elements, or to the critical eyes of people. She likens 'exposure' to the oak trees on Dartmoor which are exposed to all weathers. Exposure is painful, she says, and with *Exposure* being transparent, there is nowhere to hide. Earlier works by Wilding were often dark, hiding their contents: *Exposure* lets the interior be seen clearly, and also draws attention to its manufacture. All the time, in *Exposure*, however, the dark rubber coils counteract the notions of being transparent, of having no hiding place:

> During the construction of the piece [*Exposure*], as the sphere was being inserted into the cone, we talked about transparency allowing no hiding place – it had to be right. I liked that. But all the time I feel those dark coils which I think I feel quite close to, undoing or subverting or perhaps acting as a counterweight to transparency. (ib., 9)

Having no hiding place is a primal emotion – it is the fear of the motherless child, having nowhere to run, nowhere to be comforted. The dark coils in *Exposure* – 'which I feel quite close to' – can be seen as part of that mothering/ nurturing aspect of Wilding's sculpture. That is, the dark coils speak, as in Eva Hesse's sculpture, of a mothering, womb-like experience, a return to the Imaginary realm of Luce Irigaray and Hélène Cixous.

Wilding's cones, in *Exposure*, *Veiled*, *Ambit* and *Drowned*, are so like the rigid, upright column of the Madonna in Piero della Francesca's *Madonna della Misericordia* and *Madonna del Parto*. This column is also like the Madonna in other Renaissance pictures, where the Virgin Mary is the central pillar who upholds the meaning and emotions of the painting. In *Ambit*, it's tempting to see the bright red sphere as a creature inside the womb of the transparent cone. The red sphere speaks loudly of flesh and blood, of cells and internal organs, of mammalian life. If the red sphere in *Ambit* is ensconced inside the womb, the red sphere in Exposure is leaning or pushing out into the world, being born, perhaps, from the dark rubber coils underneath it. These biologist/ essentialist readings of Wilding's work sound ridiculous, but not unlikely. Rather, they point towards a feminist reading of

Wilding, which sees the discourse of motherhood, of sexuality and creation, of nurture and envelopment, not hidden, but openly explored.

6

Alison Wilding and Feminism

Alison Wilding's art is not obviously, blatantly, politically feminist. She does not produce highly politicized feminist work, such as Lynda Benglis, Annie Sprinkle, Kate Bornstein or Janice Perry. She is not a preacher, does not have a specific feminist agenda which she follows. Nevertheless, Wilding's art does examine notions of 'femininity', and inevitably engages with ways in which 'femininity' is represented. The very preponderance of 'feminine' imagery in Wilding's work attests to the importance of 'feminine' themes for her. The use of vessels, holes and hollows in Wilding's work puts her in the same sphere as other women artists who use vulvic/ womb imagery: Mary Beth Edelson, Judy Chicago, Niki de Sant-Phalle, etc.

Of all feminists, Wilding's sculpture is closest to the French feminism Luce Irigaray. Like Hélène Cixous, Irigaray founds much of her feminism on sexual difference, on biology, on the importance of 'female' sexuality. Like Andrea Dworkin, Susan Griffin, Catherine MacKinnon and other feminists, Irigaray foregrounds eroticism. Women have an all-over, total body eroticism, say writers such as Anais Nin, Peter Redgrove and Luce Irigaray.

'But *woman has sex organs just about everywhere.* She experiences pleasure almost everywhere' writes Irigaray.[1] This notion of an 'all-over eroticism' has affinities with sculpture, with the 'all-over' surface of sculpture, which can be so like skin. The skin is the largest external organ of the body, and is tremendously important for people's sensory awareness. Artists explore the sensitivity of skin – in obvious, dramatic ways, such as having a sheet of water falling on stage during a production of *King Lear,* for instance. Sculptors work with the body in their sculptures, their works always relate to the body, for all art is perceived by the body. As the skin is such a significant part of body-awareness, sculptors can be said to be exploring the relation between objects and skin, between the body and its awareness of touches, tastes, scents, sounds and sights. It's not far-fetched to see a heightened skin-awareness in Michelangelo, or Bernini, or Rodin, or Wilding. Every sculptor who explores notions of the body must deal with the skin, and Wilding does precisely that in sculptures such as *Jar,* where walnut wood nestles inside a casing of alabaster, or *Veiled* or *Fugue* which have an opaque outer skin which covers the inner components.

Jar is one of Wilding's most voluptuous sculptures. It is the combination of the white alabaster and the softly curved shape of an egg that suggests self-enclosed sensuousness. The title, *Jar,* and the material, alabaster, recall the beautiful pots and urns of antiquity – those of Ancient Egypt, Greece, Rome, Babylonia. Wilding's Jar, though, is distinctly 20th century. Though the egg-shape is thousands of years old – or, as a natural form, millions of years old, it is given an abstract, 20th century treatment. *Jar* is a sculpture that develops the rounded forms of Jean Arp and Constantin Brancusi. With *Jar,* Wilding continues to explore the relation between inner and outer, between something being hidden and simultaneously exposed. For inside the alabaster egg is an irregularly shaped piece of walnut wood. Embedded at the heart of the cool white alabaster egg, the black walnut also extends to the top of it, it is both inside and exposed to the outside, both skin and core.

Luce Irigaray, like French feminists such as the wonderful Hélène Cixous and Julia Kristeva, doesn't just talk of skin and 'all-over eroticism', she speaks of the vagina, of its two lips which are always embracing, so that 'woman' is not divided, she is a unity made up of an infinity of dualities. In Alison Wilding's work we see two elements who are often 'embracing'. We call her sculpture the 'sculpture of embrace' precisely because this element of nurturance, of relationship, is so important in her work. In *Dismantle*, for instance, the two elements are connected by a layer of rubber, so that the top half of the 'cone' rests gently on the lower half.

Wilding's art can be seen as 'feminist', in the sense that it explores these morphological notions of 'femininity'. Wilding's work investig-ates the volumes and spaces traditionally associated with 'femininity' (vessels, curves, wombs). This morphological/ biological description of the 'feminine' is fraught with problems, however. If we look at the critiques of Luce Irigaray's body-centred feminism we might throw some light on the sculpture of Alison Wilding, which is based, like Irigaray's feminism, on morphological/ organic/ 'natural' forms.

A good critique of Luce Irigaray's theory of female eroticism, of Irigaray's view of women's eroticism as two lips continually embracing comes from Monique Plaza, who says:

> All that 'is' woman comes to [Irigaray] in the last instances from her anatomical sex, which touches itself all the time. Poor woman.[2]

Even as Irigaray argues for a metaphysically non-representable form of female eroticism she also concentrates very much on the physicalities of female eroticism, on vaginal lips; her stance is eternally contradictory and paradoxical.[3]

Irigaray's point, as with other feminists such as Hélène Cixous, Monique Wittig and Julia Kristeva, is that women cannot be fully represented in culture, they cannot 'speak' as men do, they cannot make art as men do, because they have wombs/ vulvas/ labia, but not a phallus. The phallus is the primary signifier, the 'transcendent signifier', so important, in post-Lacanian psychoanalysis, for language and the entry into the Symbolic realm. Women must always be 'other', for they do not have the phallus. It all seems very silly, this philosophy based on the phallus. However, for many feminists, the phallus is a central part of patriarchal culture. Much patriarchal art criticism is 'phallic', preferring masculine, macho, self-aggrandizing gestures. Women artists always stand partially outside of the mainstream/ malestream art. For the French feminists, this is because 'woman' is somehow intrinsically 'other', or as Irigaray put it: '['woman'] is indefinitely other in herself,' she says.4

Luce Irigaray spoke in spatial terms of idealist feminism, and it is in terms of space that sculptors work. In reading this extract from one of Irigaray's many passages on sexual 'difference' one can fruitfully think of Wilding's sculpture:

> We need both space and time. And perhaps we are living in an age when *time must re-deploy space*. Could this be the dawning of a new world? Immanence and transcendence are being recast, notably by that threshold which has never been examined in itself: the female sex. It is a *threshold* unto mucosity. Beyond the classic opposites of love and hate, liquid and ice lies this *perpetually* half-open threshold, consisting of *lips* that are strangers to dichotomy. Pressed against one another, but without any possibility of suture, at least of a real kind, they do not absorb the world either into themselves or through themselves, provided they are not abused or reduced to a mere consummating or consuming structure. Instead their shape welcomes without assimilating or reducing or devouring. A sort of door unto voluptuousness, then? Not that, either: their useful function is to designate a *place*: the very place of uses, at least on a habitual plane. Strictly speaking, they serve neither conception nor *jouissance*. Is this, then, the mystery of female identity, of its self-contemplation, of that strange word of silence; both the threshold and reception of exchange, the

sealed-up secret of wisdom, belief and faith in every truth?[5]

Irigaray's essentialist/ biologist form of sexuality reckons that female eroticism is in some ways 'superior' to male eroticism, even though Irigaray's great feminist ethic is sexual *difference*, i.e., not 'better than', but simply 'different'; that is, not equal, but different. This is one of the primary arguments of feminist art criticism: is art by women intrinsically 'different' from that made by men? Is being a woman important in creating 'feminist' art? Or can anyone make 'feminist' art? The problem is partly that art critics and historians tend to sexualize everything, to emphasize sexuality. This is done with Alison Wilding's art, too: critics draw attention to the erotic dimension of her work, where there may be many other elements which have equal significance.

The description of sexuality in French feminism, however, has affinities with the traditional (patriarchal) view of the sensuality of sculpture. Female sexuality is an all-over eroticism, not just concentrated in the phallus, says Luce Irigaray. In a similar way, you might treat Alison Wilding's sculpture as a 'body': you might say of Wilding's *Bare*, or *Burned*, or *Temper*, that it is the whole sculpture that is significant. Not merely this bit or that bit, but every element taken together. It's a holistic mode of looking at sculpture, much as the painter Barnett Newman spoke of the 'all-over' nature of his paintings. One should not privilege this or that section of the work, but appreciate the entire work. Thus, we might speak of an æsthetic response which, as in the 'epiphany' of James Joyce, responds to the *whole artwork*. A form of total response, an æsthetics of totality. Irigaray's famous description of women's sexuality is of a total body sensuality, where the whole of the skin is alive to touches: '[t]he whole of my body is sexuate. My sexuality isn't restricted to my sex and to the sexual act (in the narrow sense)' writes Luce Irigaray (*Je, tu, nous*, 53). You might imagine a sculptor speaking in a similar way of her work: 'all of my sculpture is significant.

The æsthetic/ spiritual/ social/ ideological/ political response is not isolated to this or that area.' But Irigaray's sense of female eroticism has been criticized by feminists because it reduces women to their sexuality, it concentrates far too much on the vulva and clitoris. For some feminists, the concentration in (feminist) culture on the vulva/ vagina/ womb forgets the clitoris. The clitoris has been ignored in mainstream culture, say some feminists.[6]

The reductive nature of patriarchal art criticism, which affects Wilding just as it affects every other artist, is deadening. But, in the realm of feminist discourse, the emphasis on sexuality is, some feminists think, a drawback, because it too often speaks of only one kind of sexuality (usually heterosexual).[7] The privileging of one, monolithic, reductive form of sexuality is just as damaging as the privileging of one monolithic, reductive form of art, or, just one significant way of looking at art.

The amount of vulvic or womb imagery in women's art is interesting: it means, among other things, a reclamation and reinvention of 'feminine'/ 'female' imagery. Bombarded for centuries by images of male genitals, or images of women's genitals created by men, women artists are reclaiming their bodies. The preponderance of womb/ vulvic imagery – 'cunt art', some feminists call it – can be seen as one aspect of a feminist attempt to rewrite patriarchal notions of art. There are many examples of the phallus in art, but the vulva is curiously missing from many depictions of women by men. One sees curves, breasts, etc, in paintings by Titian and Tintoretto or sculptures by Canova or Michelangelo, but seldom the vulva. When it does appear, the vulva is often grossly misrepresented, as in Leonardo da Vinci's two bizarre drawings of the vulva. The vagina is written out of patriarchal art (except in pornography). The clitoris does not appear at all, really. When it's mentioned, patriarchy usually categorizes it as a mini-penis, that is, a substitute or tiny version of what men have. Thus, women's sexuality is defined by patriarchy always in relation to (and subordinate to) male sexuality.

Women's sexuality is often an 'absence' in patriarchal culture. The manifestation of this sexuality of 'absence', for feminists, is the womb/ vagina, which is itself absence, a hole, a vessel, something to be filled, something easily erased. It is the vagina, according to French feminists (in particular Luce Irigaray) which has been silenced, negated, decentred, written out. The penis is exalted as the emblem of presence, while the vagina is all absence. For Cixous, Irigaray et al, the vagina is a cultural hole or vacuum which cannot speak, while the phallus, the 'transcendent signifier', is all power and speech.[8] As Margaret Whitford says of Luce Irigaray's philosophy:

> Western systems of representation privilege seeing: what can be seen (presence) is privileged over what cannot be seen (absence) and guarantees Being, hence the privilege of the penis which is elevated to the status of the Phallus.[9]

Luce Irigaray sees the problem of women's art as having a genital basis: she says that if the vagina is regarded as a 'hole', it is a 'negative' space that cannot be represented in the dominant discourse. Thus to have a vagina, in the French feminist view, is to be deprived of a voice, to be decentred or culturally subordinated. So Irigaray replaces Lacan's mirror with a vaginal speculum.[10]

The evocation and exaltation of the vagina or womb in feminist/ women's art, then, is a way of countering the negation of patriarchal art. Alison Wilding, with her vulvic sculptures (*Hemlock III, Into the Dark, Immersion, Jar*, etc), can be seen as adding to this reclamation and reinvention. For Luce Irigaray, women are 'elsewhere', they are unrepresentable in patriarchal art. All we get in patriarchy is the reflection of patriarchal negativity, in Irigaray's feminist notion of specularization.[11] Wilding' vaginal sculptures, however, are very definitely *there*, they assert their presence in a space very powerfully. Even though they are not large, space-dominating works such as those by Richard Serra, Walter de Maria, Christo, Tony Cragg or George Segal, they assert themselves author-itatively.

For Luce Irigaray, 'woman' exists in some forbidden space, an in-between space, 'in between signs, between the realized meanings, between the lines',[11] she writes. The hope is that there is still a truly 'feminine' space, the 'wild zone' of feminists such as Elaine Showalter and Jeanne Roberts. The male 'wild zone' we know about, it's on the edges of Western culture, that masculine version of wild zone eroticism which Hélène Cixous calls 'glorious phallic monosexuality'.[13] The female 'wild zone', on the other hand, is beyond patriarchal space, beyond patriarchal representations. Julia Kristeva and Luce Irigaray have spoken of something in 'women' or the 'feminine' that is 'unrepresentable', beyond art, beyond male culture. Victor Burgin, describing Julia Kristeva's philosophy,[14] says that she positions

> the woman in society... in the patriarchal scheme, as perpetually at the boundary, the borderline, the edge, the 'outer limit' – the place where order shades into chaos, light into darkness. This peripheral and ambivalent position allocated to woman, says Kristeva, had led to that familiar division of the field of representation in which women are viewed as either saintly or demonic – according to whether they are seen as bringing the darkness, or as keeping it out.

We know about these stereotypes or archetypes, these saintly women (the Virgin Mary is a typical example) who keep the amazing energy of the female wild zone out of men's lives. The demonic woman (Mary Magdalene, the *femme fatale*, vampire, 'devil woman') is the one who brings the wildness with her, and is, of course, feared (and desired) and suppressed by patriarchy. For patriarchy of course prefers bland, mute, passive door-stops in women, people who will stop the darkness from coming in, who will sit there and say nothing and get on with society's housework. Alison Wilding's art shows that 'woman'/ the 'feminine'/

'womanhood' is not about domesticity necessarily, or doing chores, or stereotypes, or dualities of good/ evil, saints/ sinners. Wilding's sculpture demonstrates that notions of 'femininity', like 'feminism', are continually changing. The very ambiguity and unfixedness of Wilding's art shows how important the sense of change and fluidity is for her. Wilding uses materials that will change over time (beeswax, wood, lime), materials that are not 'permanent'. Sculptors such as Rebecca Horn and Alice Aycock actively encourage a sense of time and change. Andy Goldsworthy, Mary Miss, David Nash and Richard Long make sculptures that don't 'last': some of them don't even last minutes. When Andy Goldsworthy's arches crumble, he takes pictures of them collapsing – he enjoys the moment of destruction. Wilding, too, enjoys the changes in her sculptures. The sense of change means that Wilding's sculpture will not be locked down to one form of feminism, to one feminist reading, to one feminist/ non-feminist philosophy. The fluidity of Wilding's forms also shows that her art will not be fixed to one spatiality, one morphology, one set of organic/ biological/ 'natural' interpretations. Wilding does not, like Luce Irigaray, make all her explorations pivot on a single biological reality, the labial lips embracing. However much the womb or labia is significant for (French) feminists, Wilding will not be so reductive in her art. Her sense of feminist art must include generous helpings of ambiguity, change, mystery, openness and instability.

Illustrations

by Alison Wilding,
and some of her contemporaries

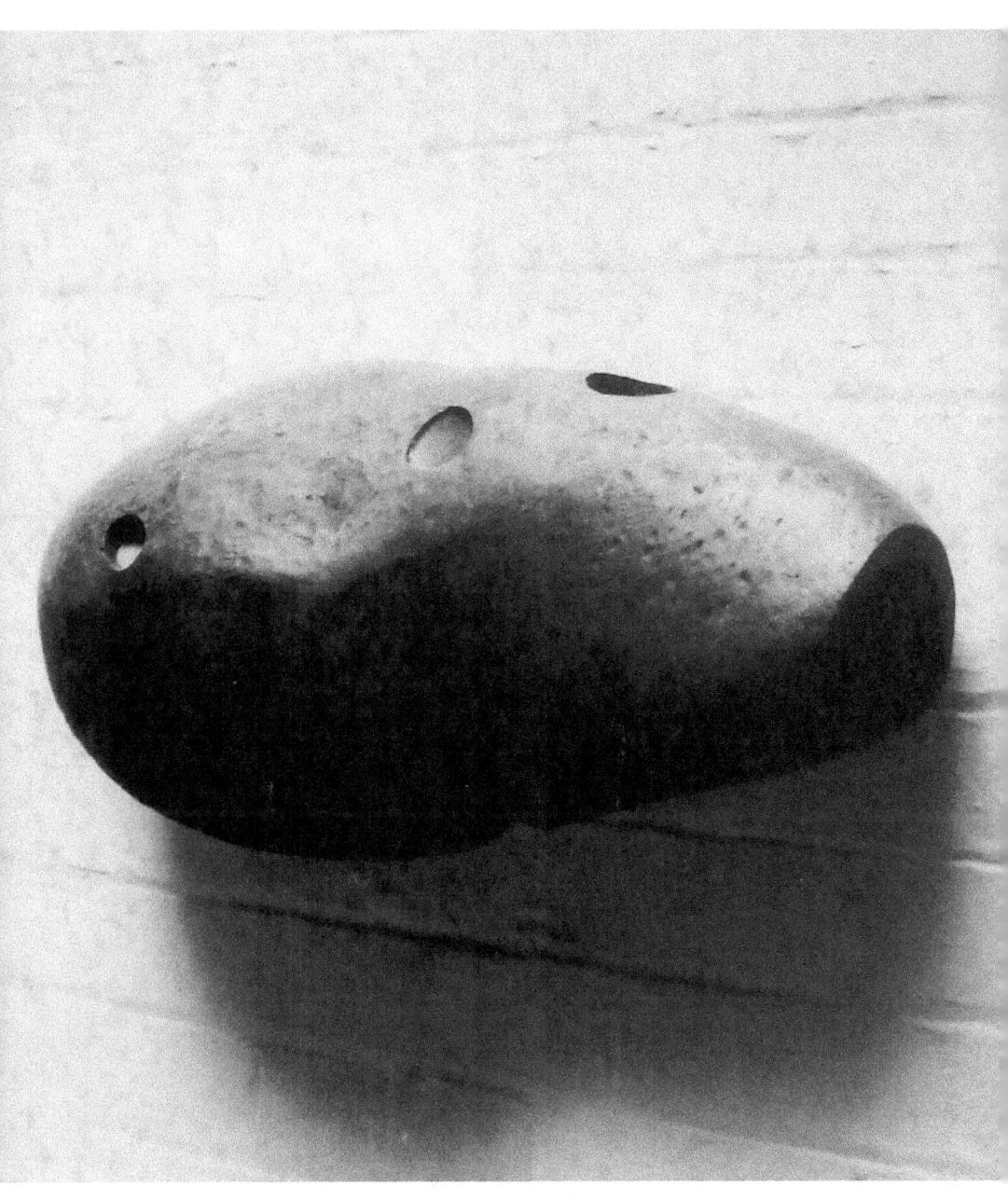

Alison Wilding, Beneath the Skin, 1986

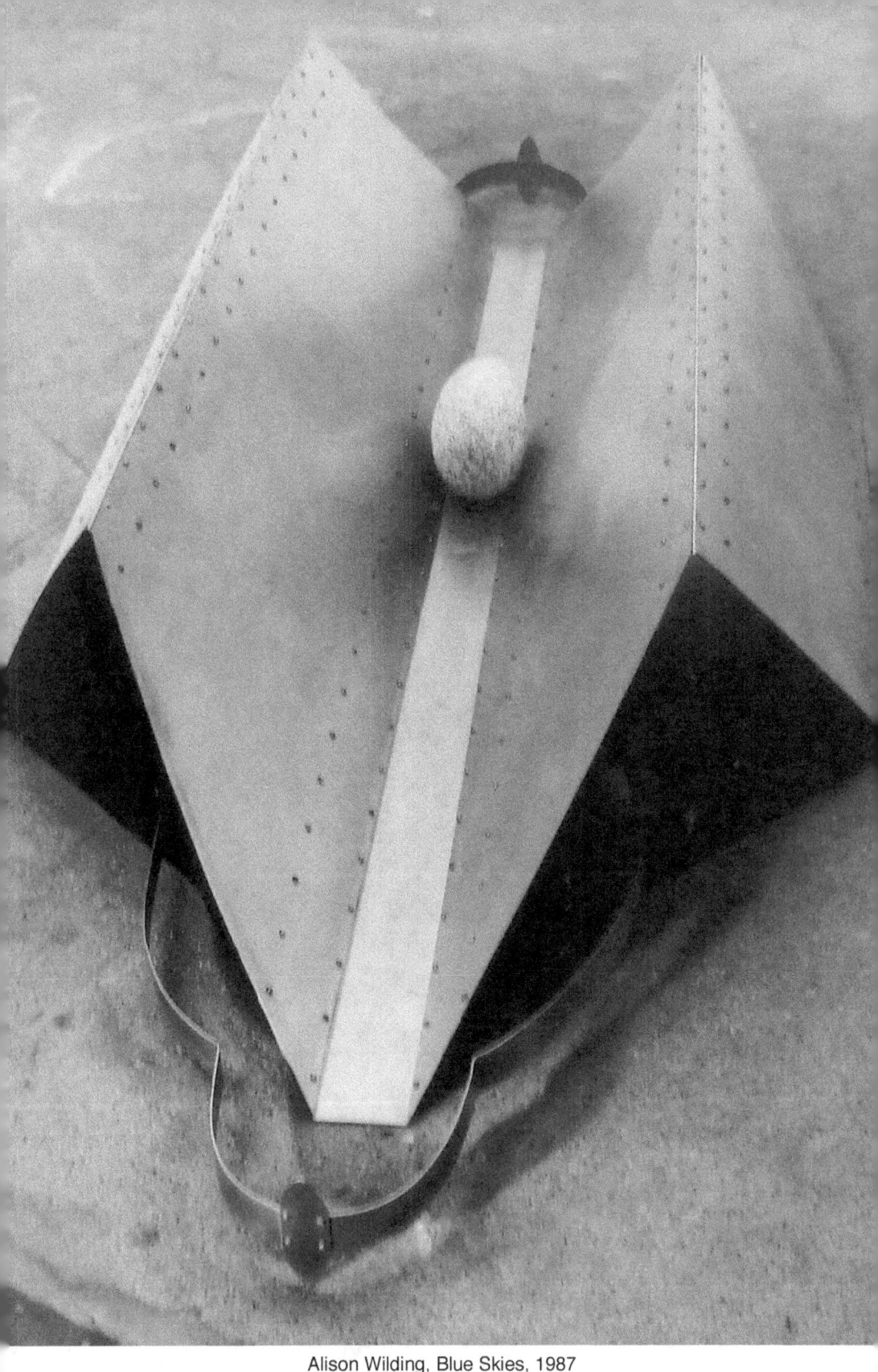

Alison Wilding, Blue Skies, 1987

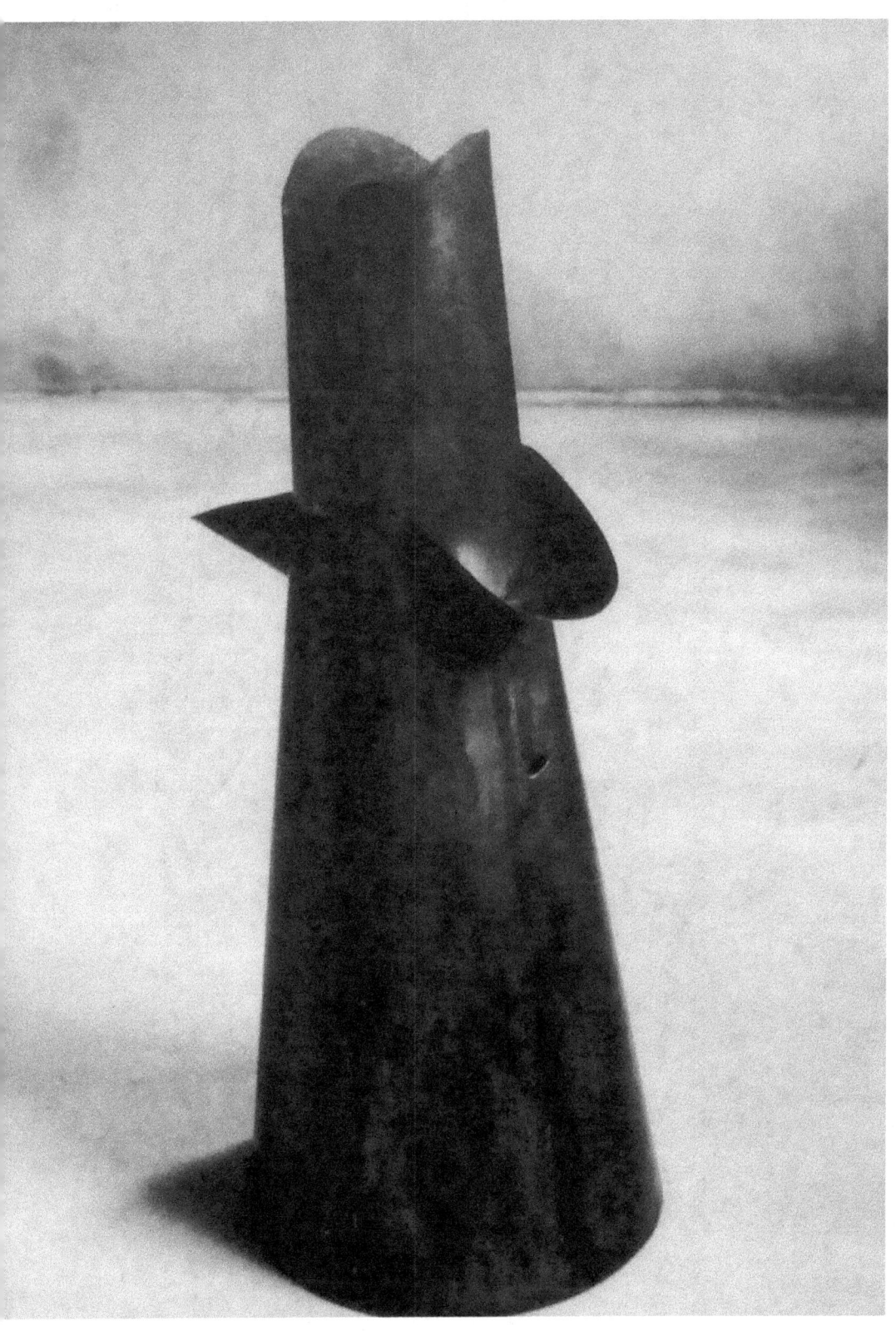

Alision Wilding, Her Furnace, 1986-76

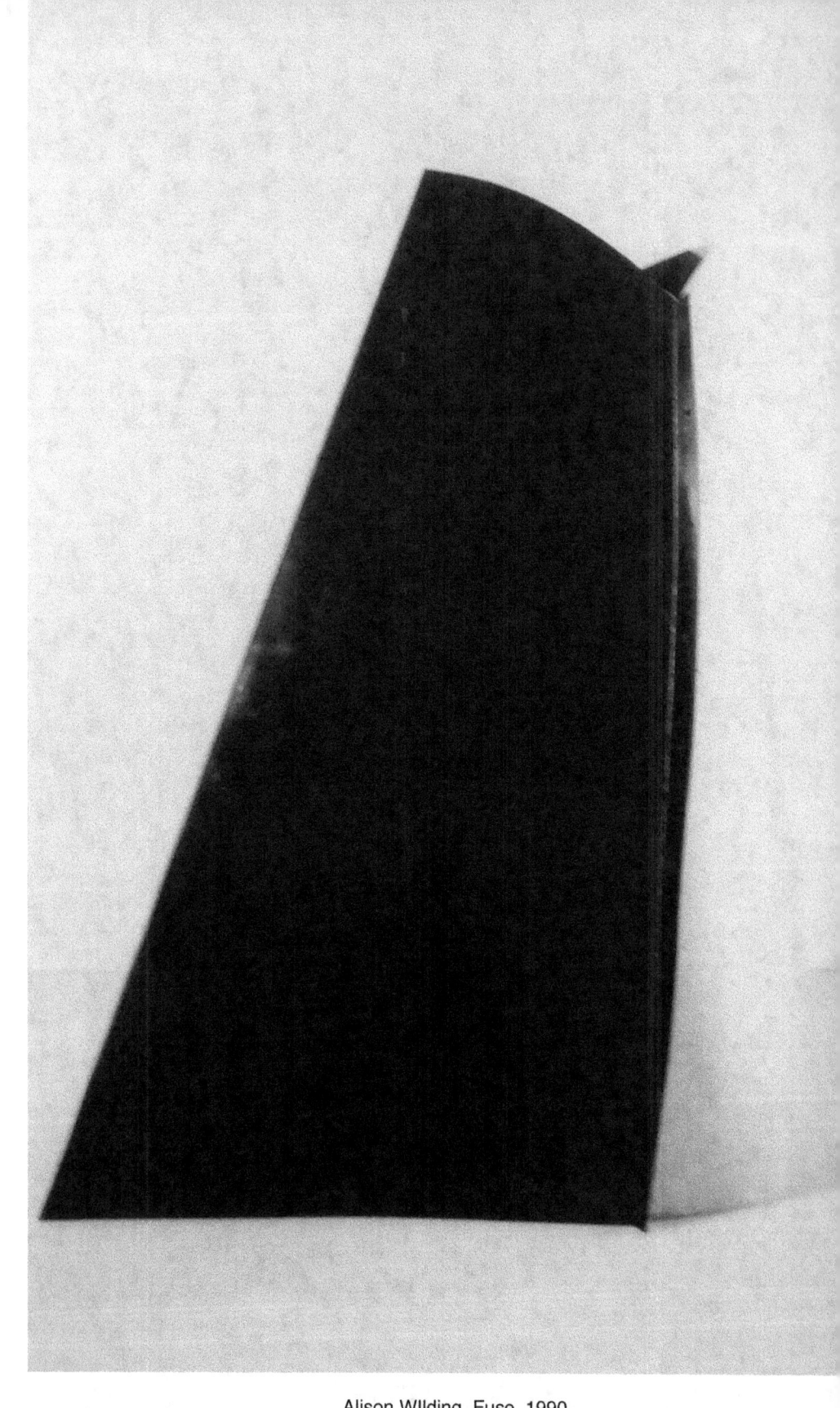

Alison WIlding, Fuse, 1990

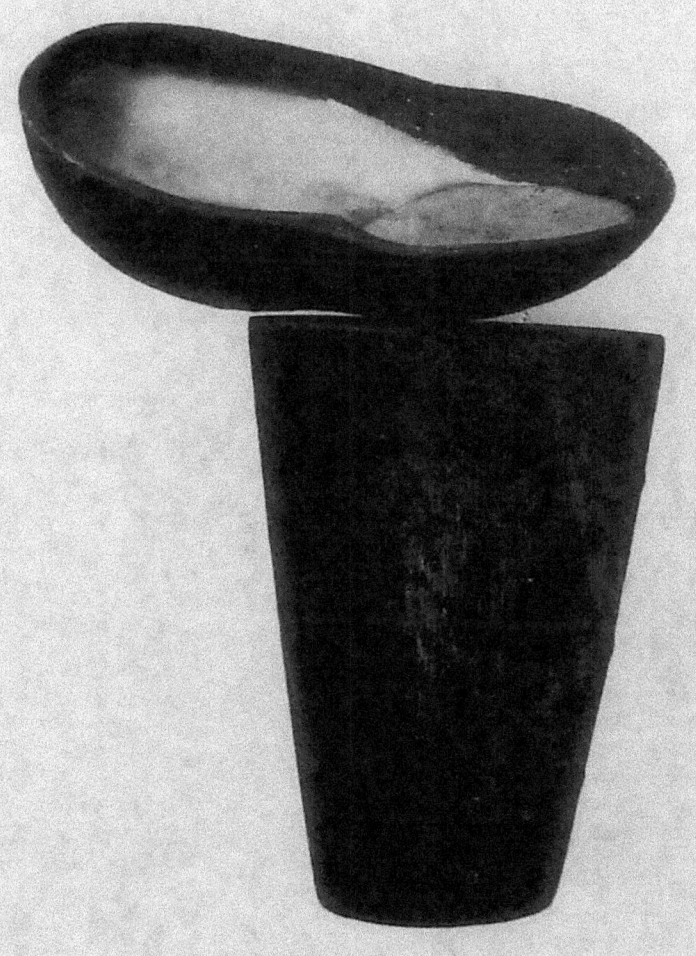

Alison Wilding, Hemlock III, 1986

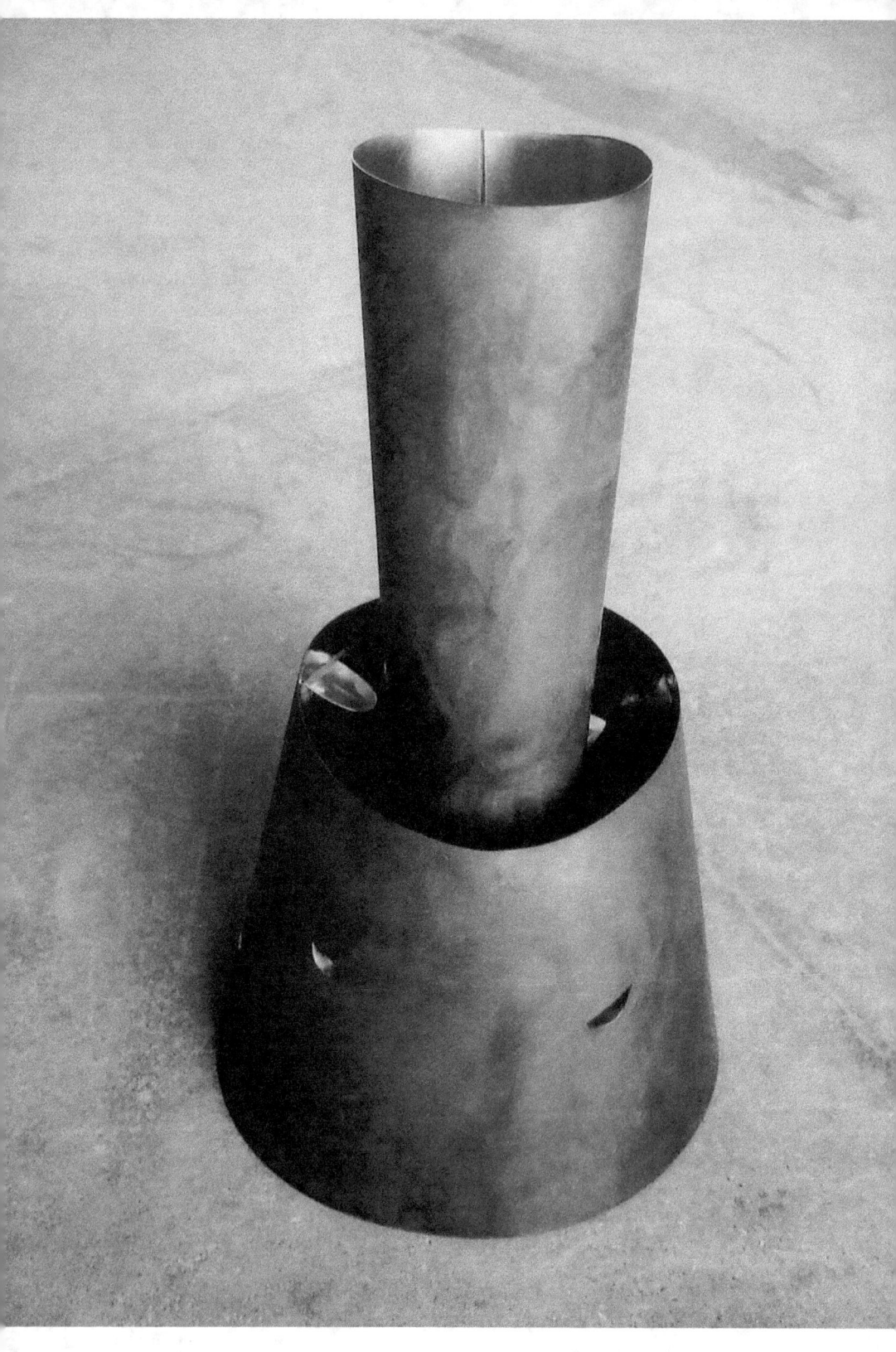

Alison Wilding, Immersion, 1988

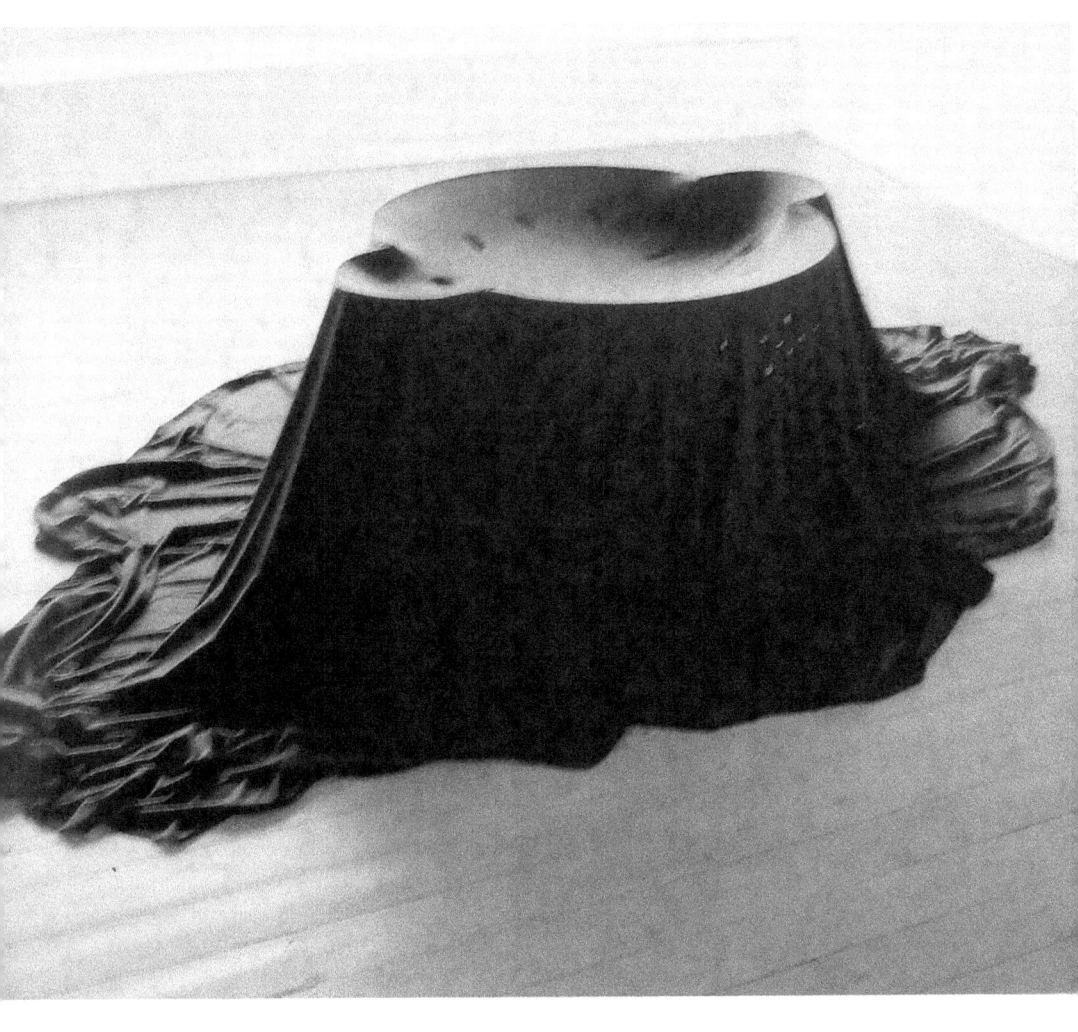

Alision Wilding, Into the brass, 1987

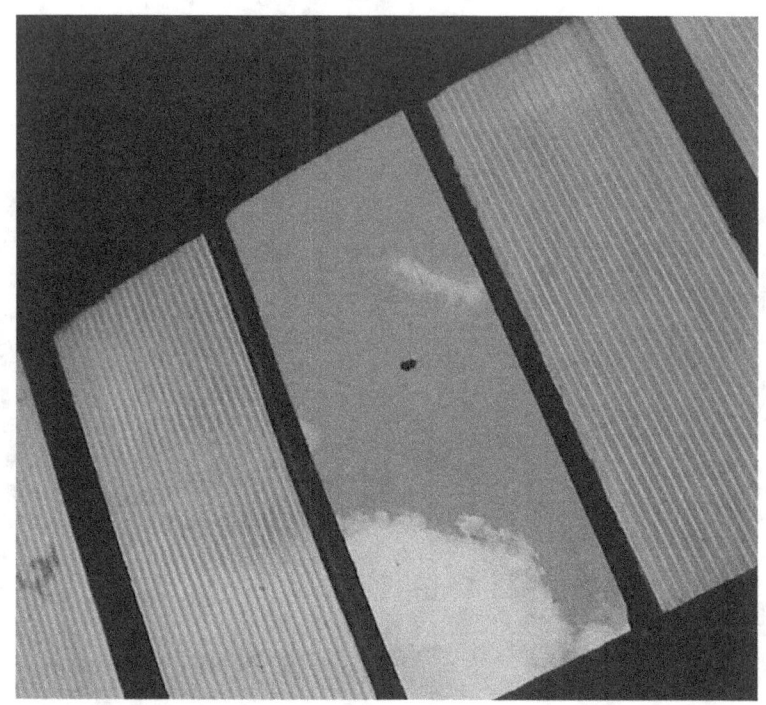

Alison Wilding, Iron Meteroite

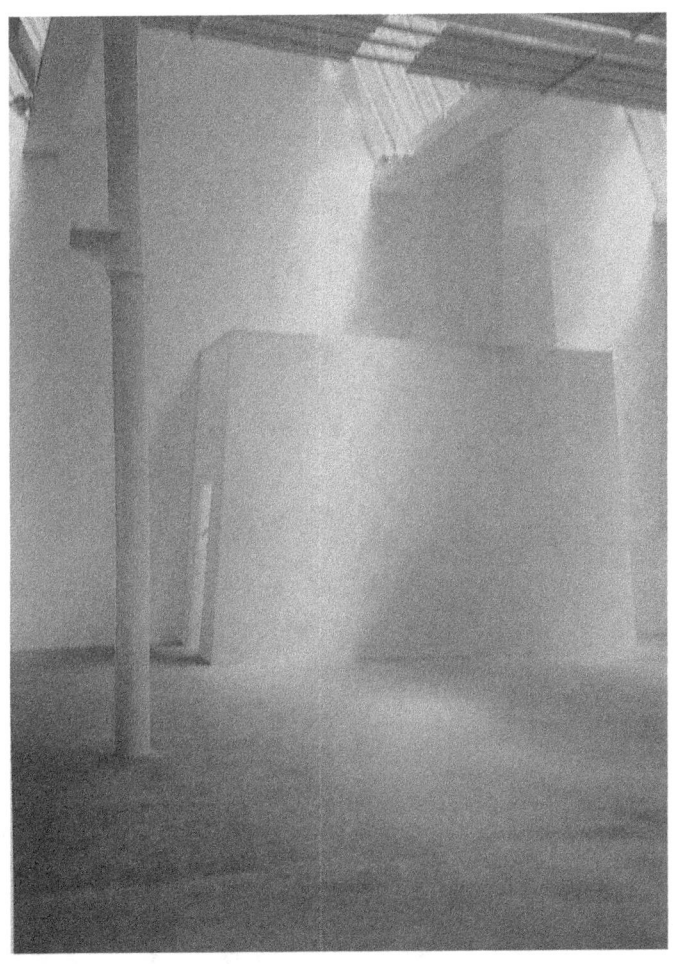

Alison Wilding, Pulse, 1991

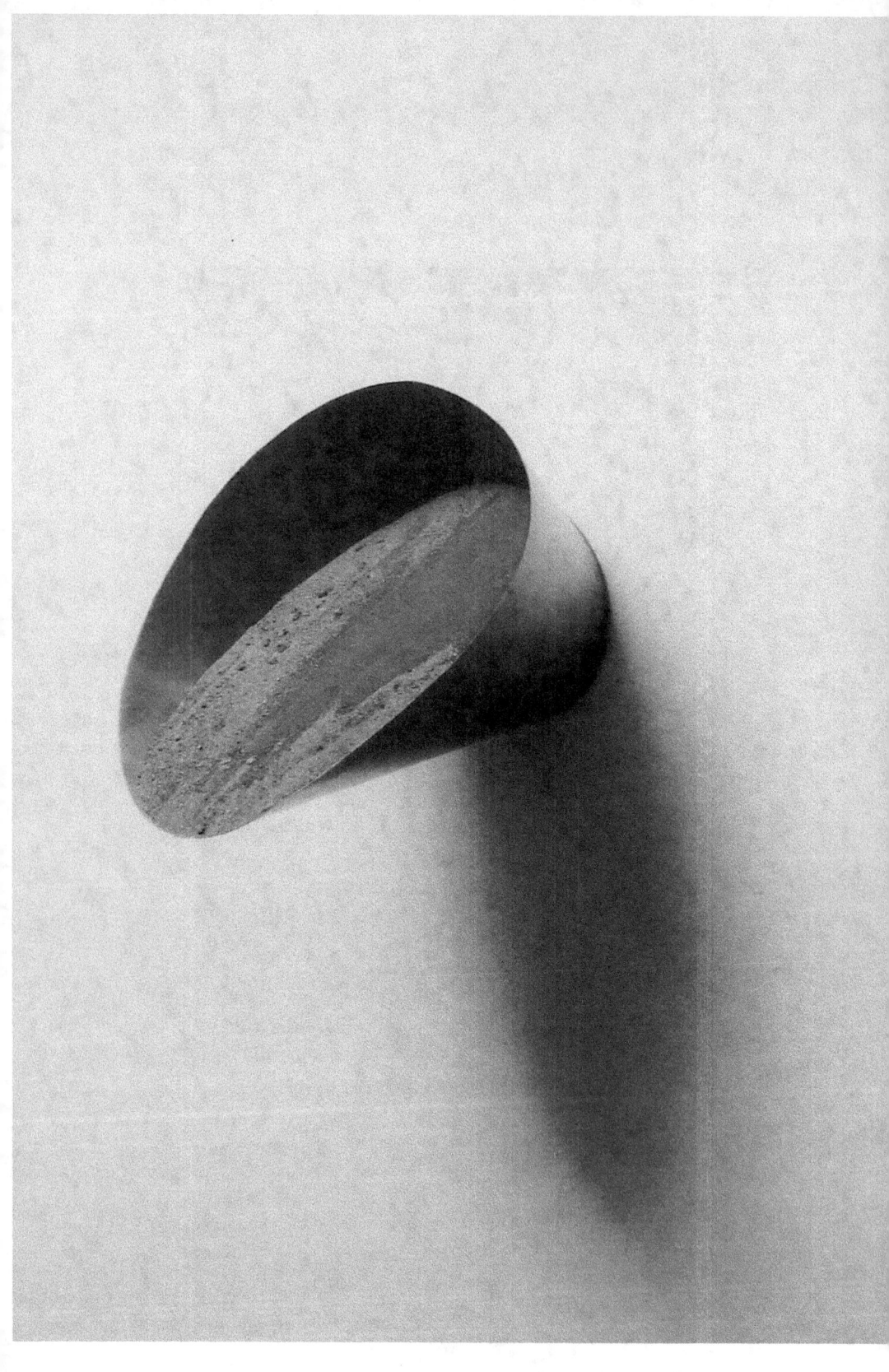

Alison Wilding, Scree, 1984

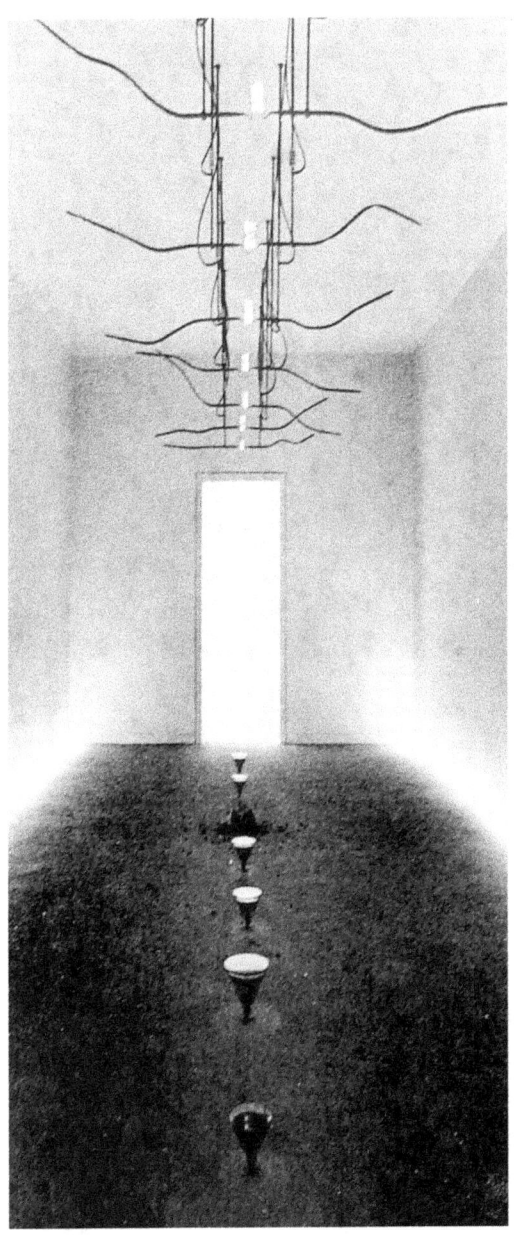

Rebecca Horn

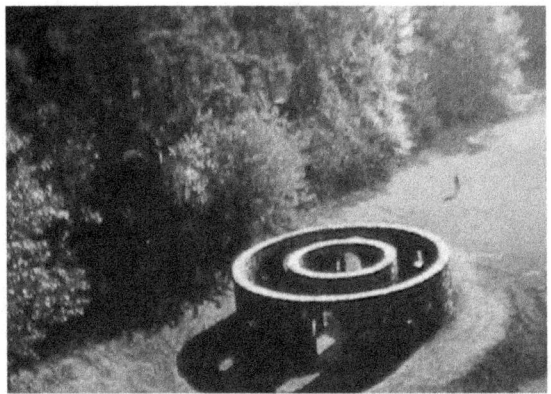

Nancy Holt, Stone Enclosure - Rock Rings, 1977-78

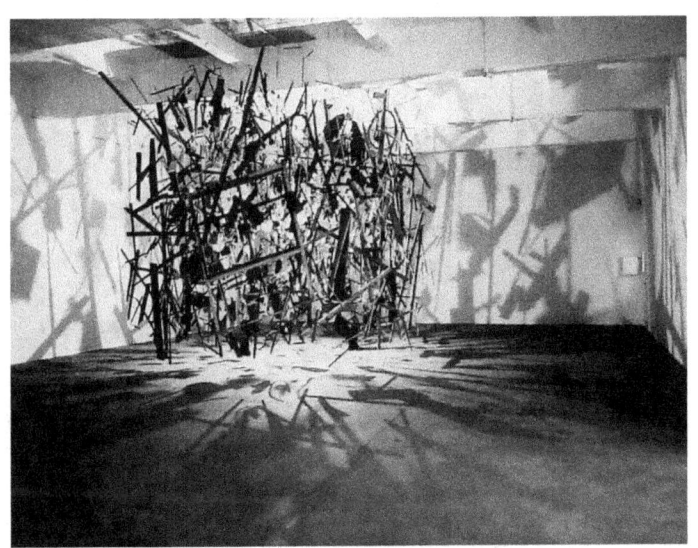

Cornelia Parker

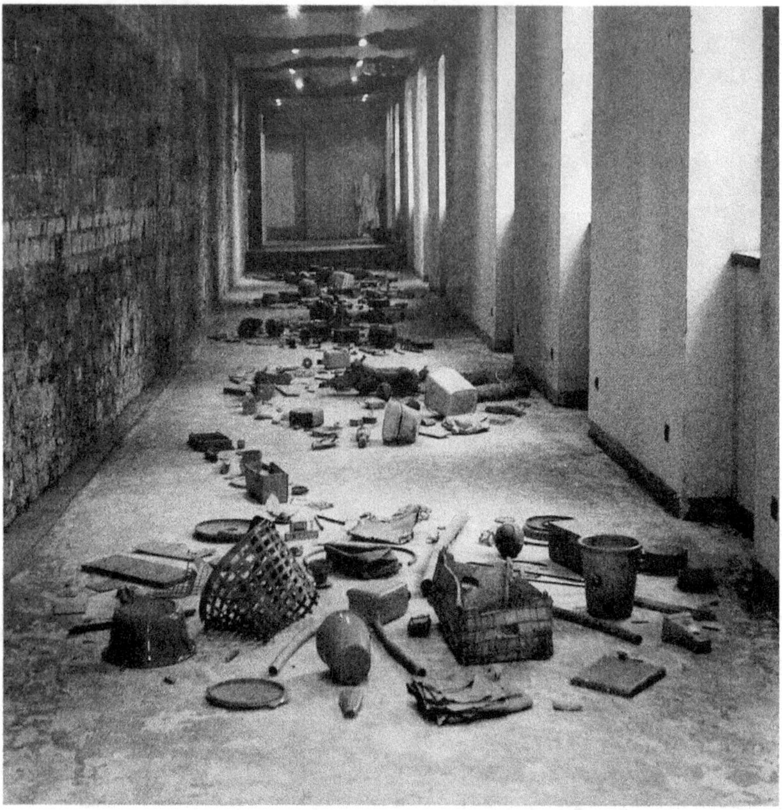

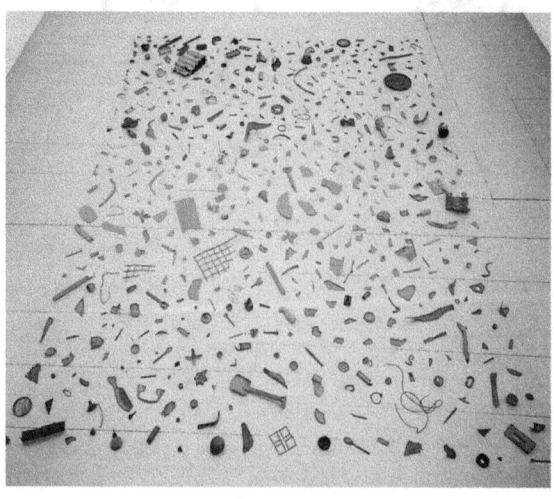

Tony Cragg

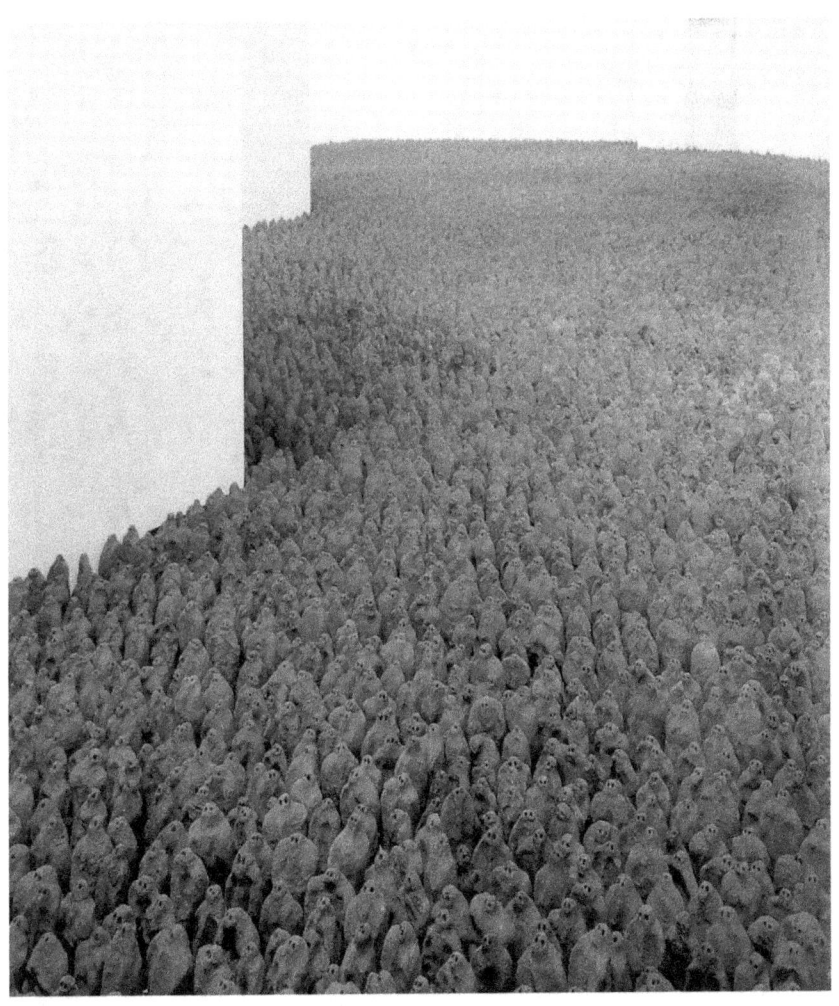

Anthony Gormley

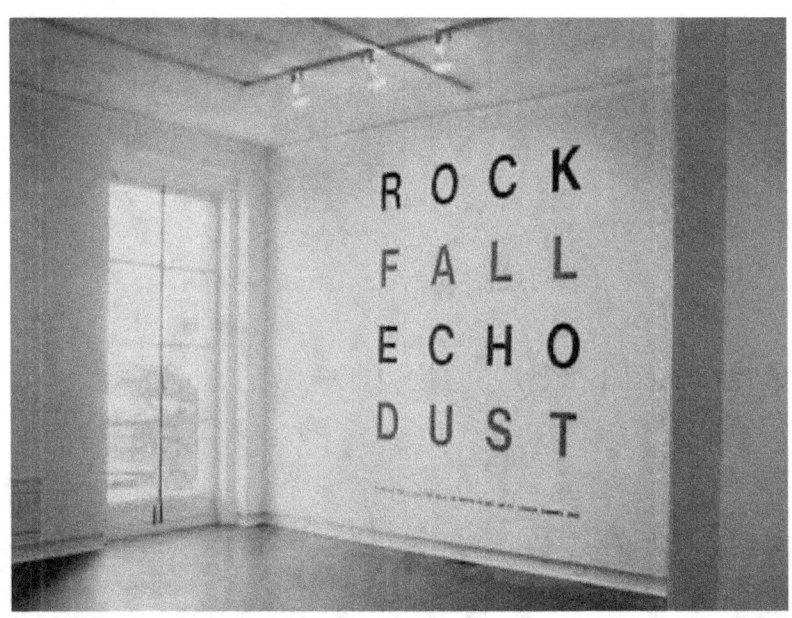

Hamish Fulton

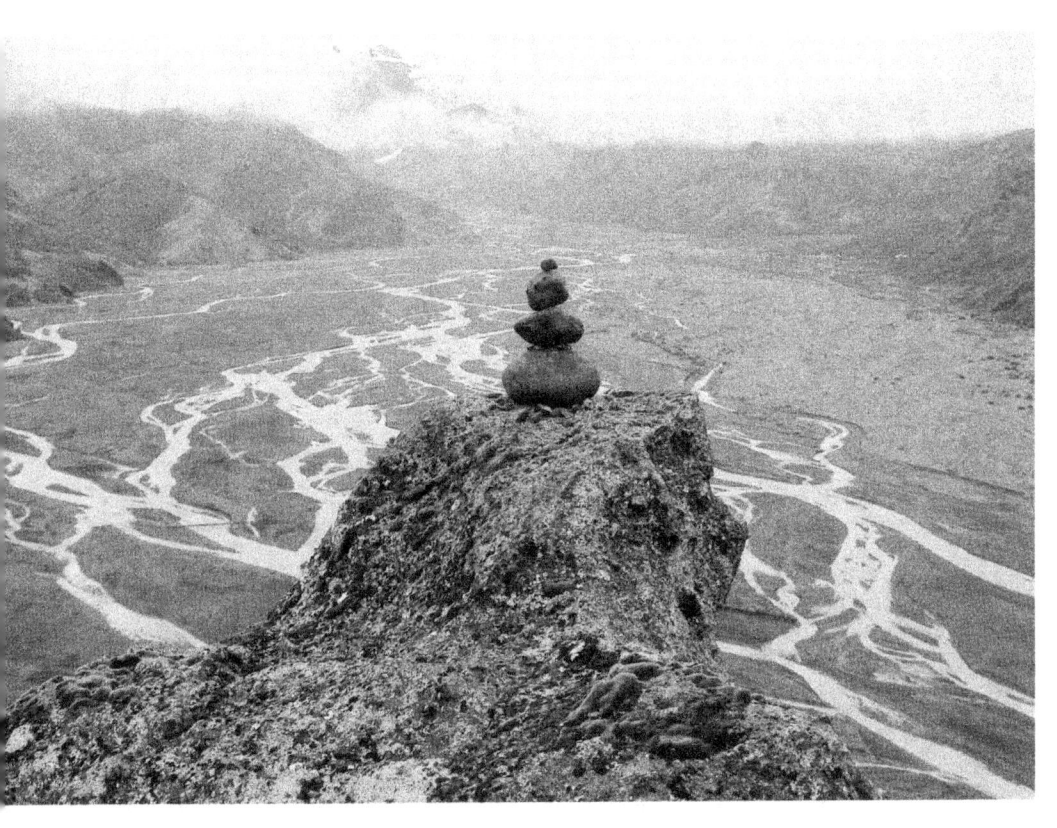

Chris Drury, Cairn

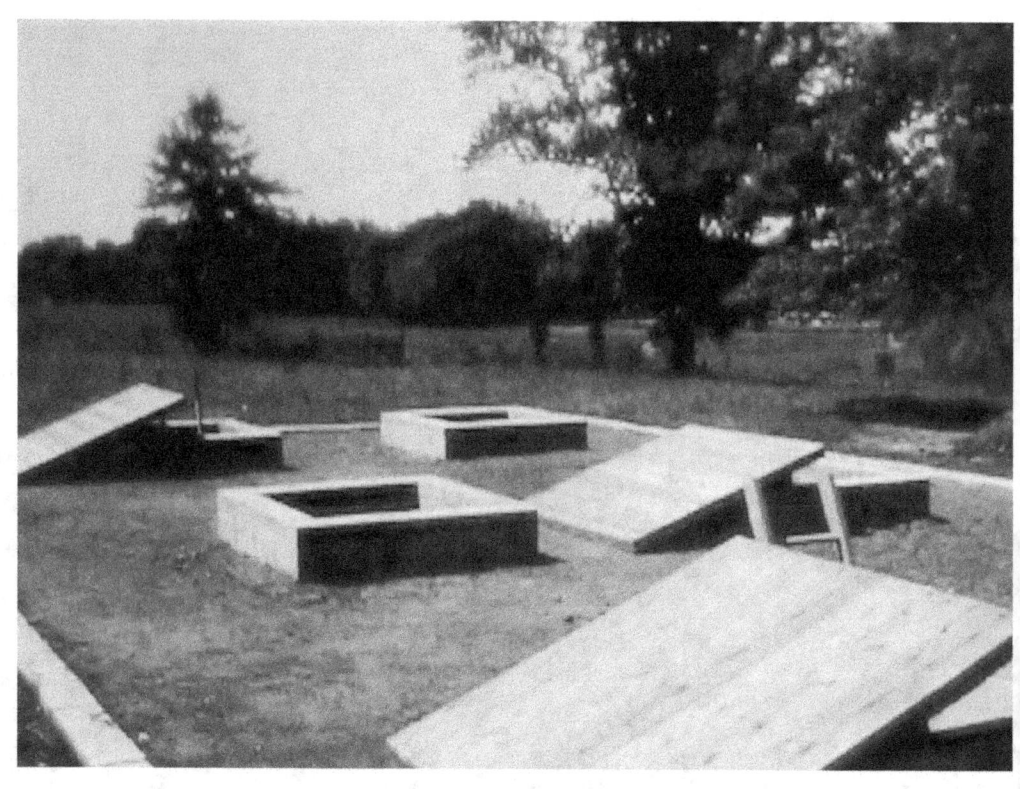

Alice Aycock, A Simple Network of Underground
Walls and Tunnels, 1975

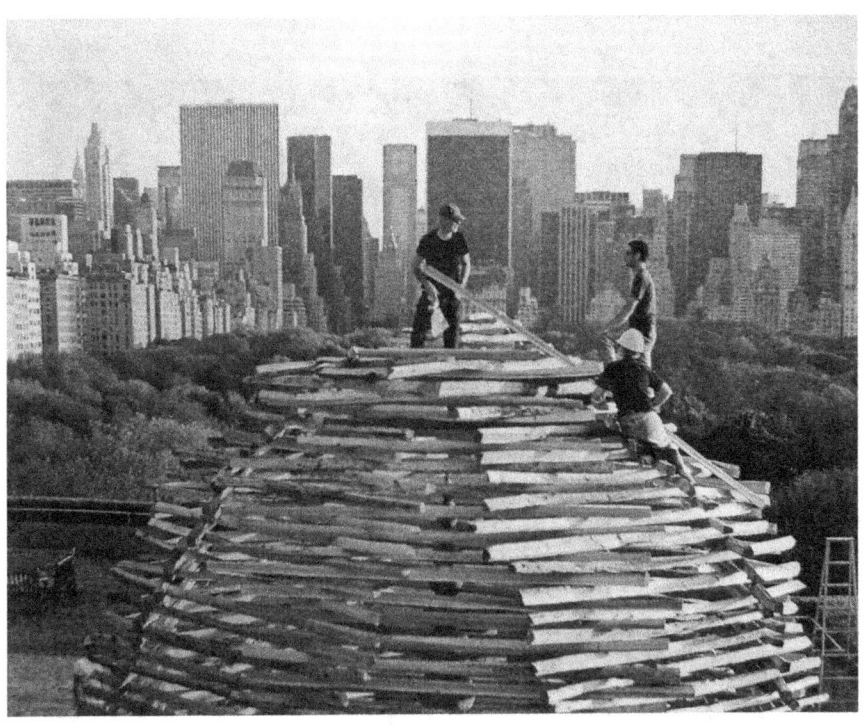

Andy Goldsworthy, Garden of Stones, New York City, 2003

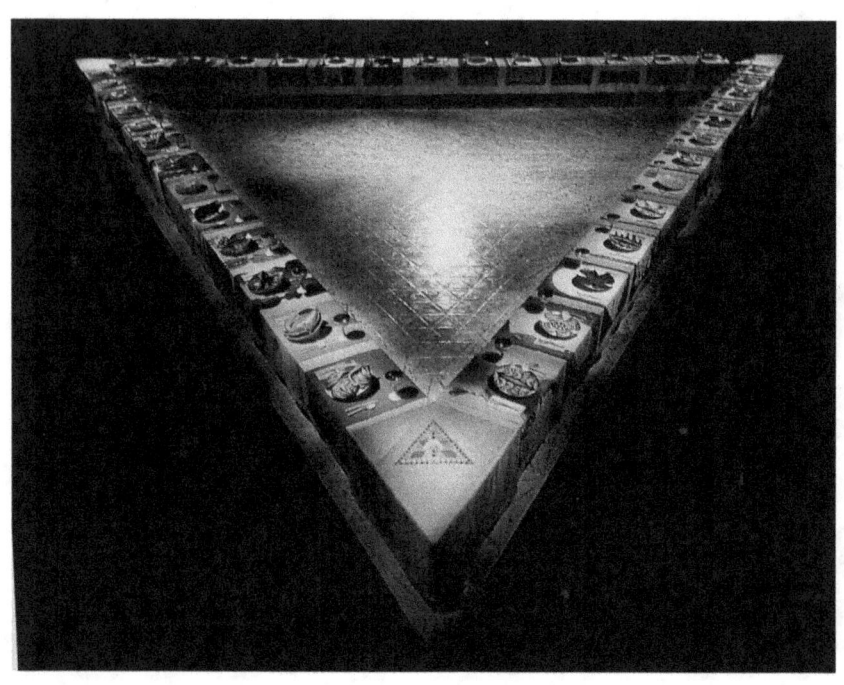

Judy Chicago

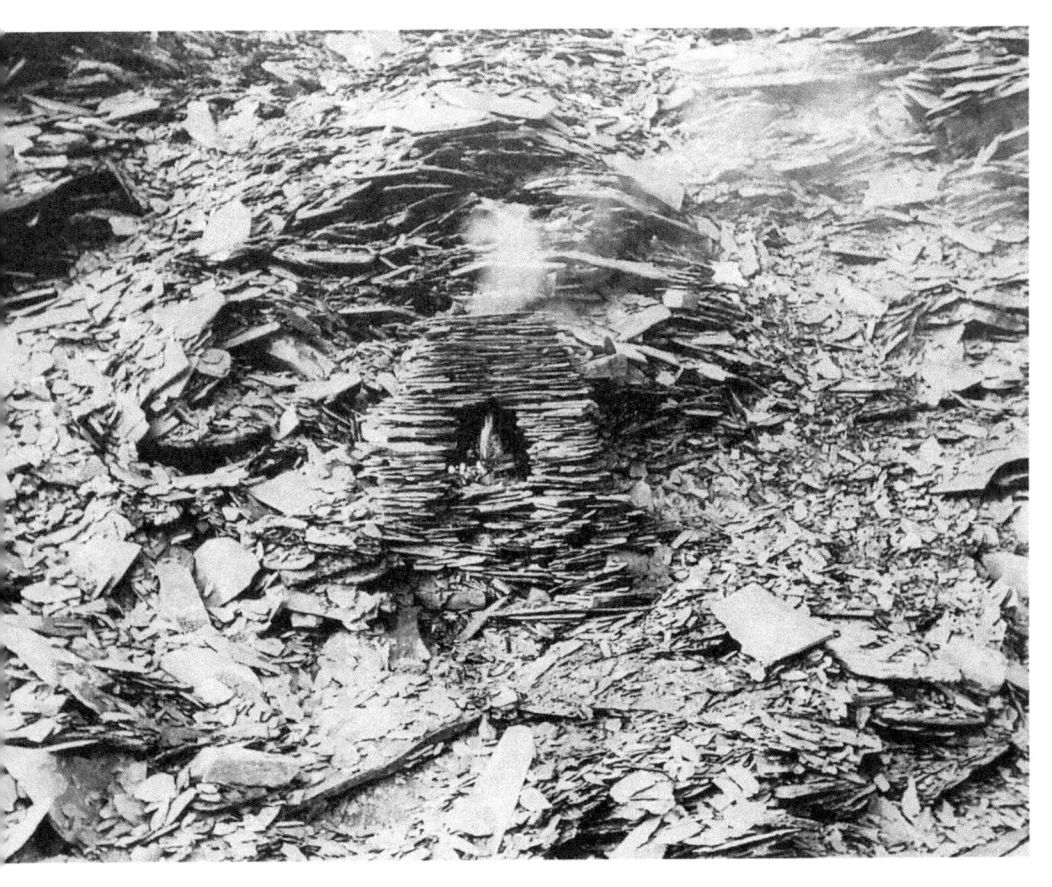

David Nash

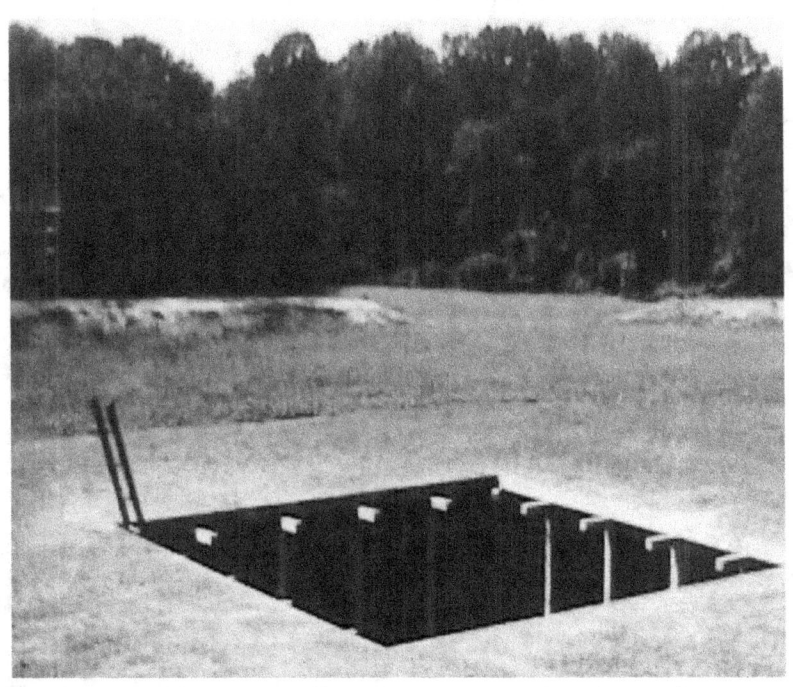

Mary Miss, Perimeters/ Pavilion/ Decoys. 1978

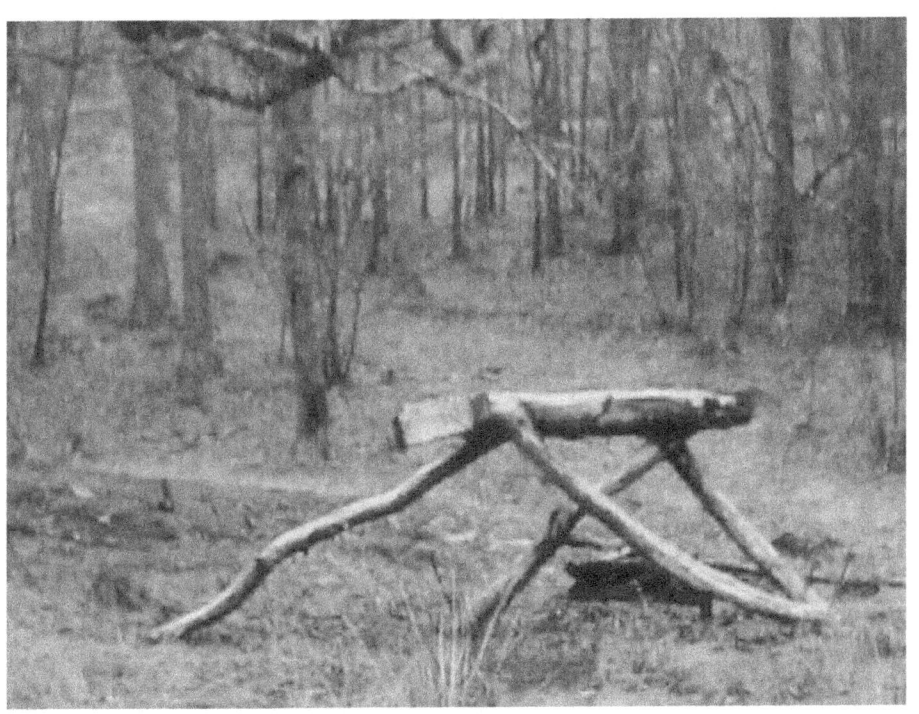

David Nash

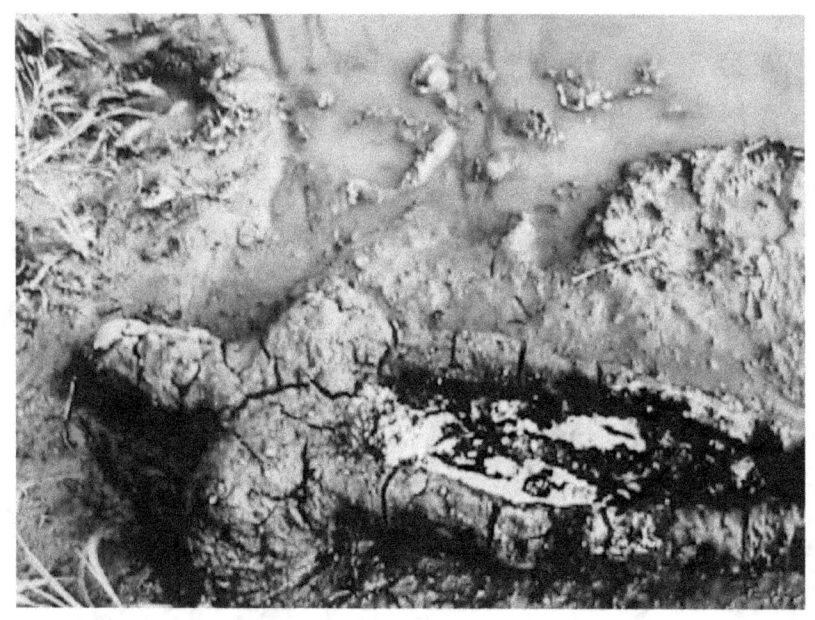

Ana Mendieta, Silueta Series, 1979

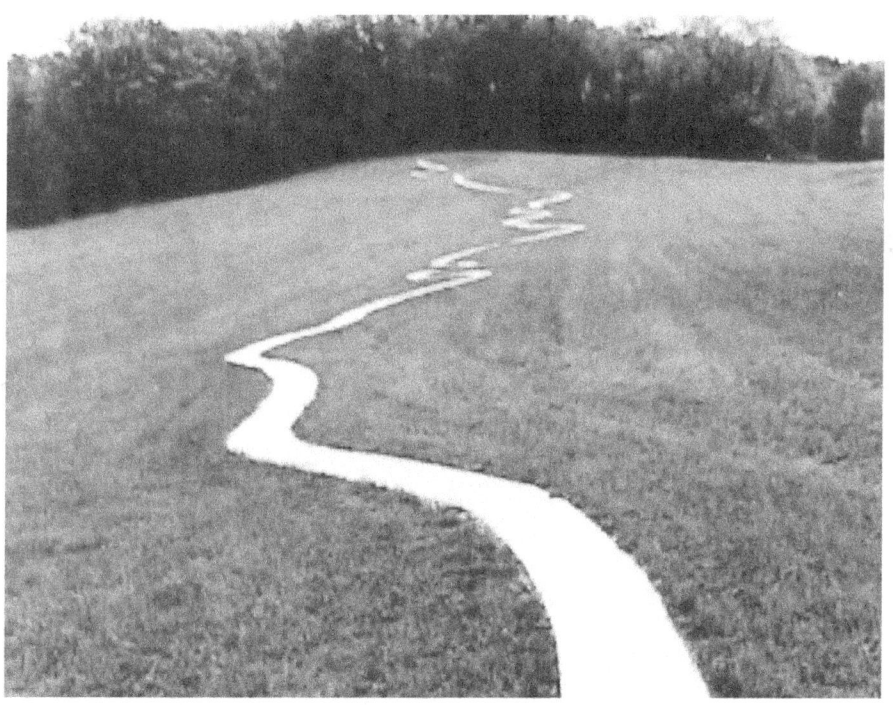

Richard Long, River Po Line, 2001

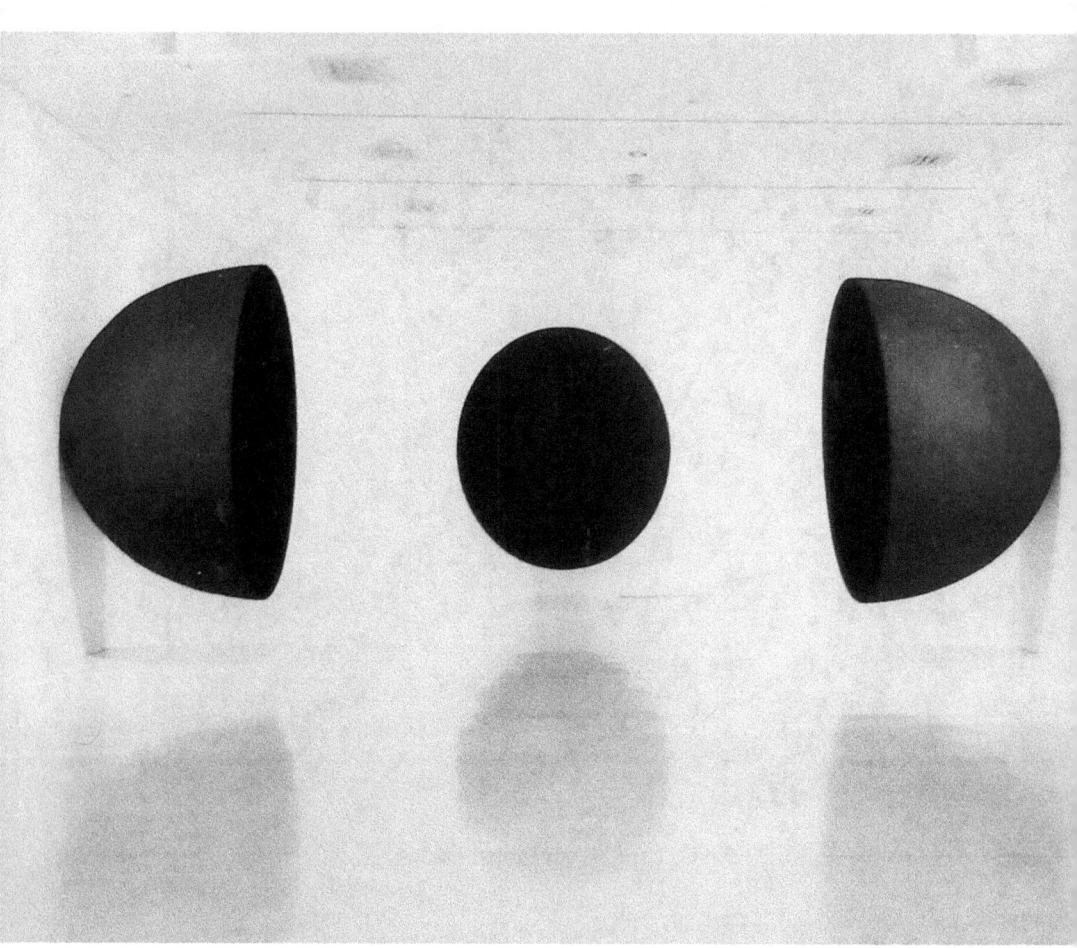

Anish Kapoor

A list of some works cited

Ambit, 1993-4, The Mattress Factory, Pittsburgh

Bare, 1989-90, patinated brass, copper tube & braid, 51 x 55.5 x 52.5 in, collection: Richard Salmon, London

Beneath the Skin, 1986, wood & wax, 28.5 x 67.3 x 12.7 cm, collection: Martin Kunz, New York

Blueblack, 1984, lime & elm woods, wax, lead, 36 x 28 x 49cm, collection: the artist

Blue Skies, 1987, galvanized steel, granite & nickel silver, 50 x 284 x 132 cm, Southampton City Art Gallery

Brim, 1984, lead, oil paint, steel & granite, 13.5 x 30.3 x 14. 5 in, collection: Richard Salmon, London

Burned, 1992, copper wire, each 65 x 19 x 13 in, collection: Ed Broida Trust, Los Angeles

Crown I, 1994, copper & brass, 31 x 19 x 7.5 cm, private collection

Curvature, 1985, leaded steel, chestnut, wax, pigment, 79 x 155 x 244 cm, Arts Council

Deep, 1984, ash, galvanised steel, oil paint, 207 x 99 x 52cm, Arts Council

Dismantle, 1990, fibreglass resin, rubber & oil paint on leaded steel, 120 x 35 x 53 in, collection: William Louis-Dreyfus, New York

Displace, 1990, polypropylene, steel & rubber, 218.4 x 193 x 97.8 cm, Karsten Schubert

Exposure, 1993, Tate Galery, St Ives

Fruit, 1990, tektite & brass, 101 x 101 x 89mm, private collection

Fugue, 1992, polypropylene, brass, lead & wax, 82.7 x 48 x 48 in, Karsten Schubert

Fuse, 1990, polypropylene & leaded steel, 177.8 x 121.9 x 175.3 cm, Karsten Schubert

Green Beak, 1983, slate & copper, 14 x 58 x 16cm, Arts Council Collection

Hard for Hard, 1984, Belgian fossil, brass, 35 x 160 x 115 cm, Arts Council
Hearth, 1986, copper, brass, leaded steel & pigment, 208.5 x 40.7 x 96.5 cm, private collection
Hemlock II, 1982, brass, wax & hemlock, 3.8 x 24 x 3.8 in, private collection
Hemlock III, 1986, lime, hemlock, lead, beeswax, pigment, Karsten Schubert
Her Furnace, 1986-7, brass & copper, 86.5 x 39.5 x 25.5 cm, private collection
Immersion, 1988, brass, 99.7 x 48.3 x 55.9 cm, Edward Broida Trust
Indelible Field, 1984, graphite, oak, brass, copper, 35 x 216x 282cm, Arts Council
Infinities, 1991, meteorite cast in bronze set in resin cast from potato, 10.7 x 6.5 x 4.5 cm
Inland, 1990, polypropylene, 70.3 x 47.3 x 47.3 in, Karsten Schubert
Into the Brass, 1987, brass & wool/ cotton cloth, 91 x 205 x 123 cm, private collection
Into the Dark, 1986, limewood, lead & pigment, collection: Richard Salmon, London
Jar, 1992-3, black walnut & alabaster, 11.8 x 8.8. x 4.8 in, Karsten Schubert
Locust, 1983, wood, wax, copper, 208 x 71 x 46cm, collection: the artist
Meridan II, 1994, copper, brass & polyester resin, 11 x 99.5 x 4.2 cm, private collection
Nature: Blue and Gold, 1984, brass, ash, oil & pigment, 47 x 109 x 22cm, British Council Collection
Nest, 1986, Issore marble & copper, 60 x 32.5 x 32 cm, private collection
Orbit II, 1994, brass & copper, 21 x 21 x 15 cm, private collection
Pair I, 1994-5, copper, brass & silver solder, each 55 x 18.5 x 10 cm, private collection
Pond, 1983, copper, slate & Portland roach, 26.5 x 180 cm diameter, collection: the artist
Possession, 1989, utile wax, oak & oil, 31.1 x 68.6 x 23.5 cm, private collection
Pulse, 1991, polypropylene, 585.5 x 543 x 214.5 cm, installation
Receiver, 1988, steel, pigment, beeswax & oak, 194.5 x 140.5 x 100 cm, Karsten Schubert
Scree, 1983, slate & patinated copper, 58 x 16 x 14 cm, Arts Council Collection
Seal, 1990, polypropylene, stone
Stain, 1991, steel, rubber, woollen cloth, 297 x 1000 x 485 cm, private collection
Stormy Weather, 1987, steel, oil & bronze, 224.8 x 115. 6 x 170.2 cm, Weltkunst Foundation, Zurich
Tidal, 1990-1, brass, rubber & steel, 184 x 226 x 79, collection: the artist
Untitled, 1980, Arts Council of Great Britain, London
Untitled, 1981, silk, copper & wood, 50.8 x 10.2 x 10.2 cm, private collection
Veiled No 2, 1993, Tate Gallery, St Ives
Vestal, 1985, brass, 42 x 15.4 x 17.3 in, collection: William Louis-Dreyfus, New York
Well, 1985, limewood, paint & leaded steel, 40 x 29.2 x 14 cm, collection: Cosmo Rodewald

Notes

1 : Introduction

1. Peter Fuller, *Peter Fuller's Modern Painters: Reflections on British Art,* ed John McDonald, Methuen 1993
2. Kent C. Bloomert, 34; see also James Gibson
3. Ash, in Wilding, *Bare,* 5

2 : Alison Wilding and Women Sculptors

1. Hepworth: quoted in A.M. Hammacher: T*he Sculpture of Barbara Hepworth,* Abrams, New York 1968, 99
2. Crichton: "When form engenders attitude", in de Monchaux, 1983, 57
3. Richard Long: *Richard Long: In Conversation,* Parts 1 & 2, MW Press, Noordwijk, Holland 1985-6 2, 21
4. Deacon, quoted in the video for *Entre el Objeto,* Palacio de Velasquez, Madrid, 1986
5. see Bill Barrette: *Eva Hesse's Sculpture: Catalogue Raisonne,* New York 1989, Rosalind Krauss & Eva Hesse: *Eva Hesse: Sculpture,* Whitechapel Art Gallery 1979; Cindy Nemser: "My Memories of Eva Hesse", *Feminist Art Journal,* Winter 1973, 12-3
6. Eva Hesse: *Contingent,* 1969, reinforced fibreglass and latex over cheesecloth, each of 8 units, 9.5-14 x 3-4ft, Australian National Gallery, Canberra; *Aught,* 1968, double sheets of latex rubber, polyethylene plastic inside, 4 units, each 78 in high, collection: the artist; *Ice Piece,* 1969, fibreglass and wire, 62 x 1 in, Xavier Fourcade Gallery, New York
7. Cindy Nemser: "An interview with Eva Hesse", *Artforum,* May 1970, 62
8. Daniel Wheeler, 259
9. Hesse, in *Eva Hesse,* Guggenheim, New York 1972
10. Jackie Winsor: *Installation,* 1982, mixed media, Paula Cooper Gallery, New

York

11. Hilton Kramer, *New York Times,* 1979, in Lucie-Smith, 1987, 115

12. Winsor, in Wheeler, 323

13. Barbara Rose: "New York Letter", *Art International,* 15 Feb 1964, 41

14. Robert Morris: "Notes on Sculpture", *Artforum,* October 1966, 20-3. See also: Phil Patton: "Robert Morris and the Fire Next Time", *Art News,* vol.82, no.10, December 1983, 84-91

15. see Irving Sandler, *American Art,* 245f, Lucy Lippard: "An Impure Situation", *Art International,* 20 May 1966, 62, Robert Morris: "Notes on Sculpture", op.cit., Kynaston McShine: *Primary Structures,* Jewish Museum, New York 1966, Richard Lund: "Why Isn't Minimal Art Boring?", *Journal of Aesthetics and Art Criticism,* vol.45, no.2, Winter 1986, 195-7

16. Lucy Lippard: "New York Letter: Recent Sculpture as Escape", *Art International,* Feb 1966, 50

17. Judd: "Questions to Stella and Judd", in Battock, 159

18. James Mellow: "New York Letter", *Art International,* 20 April 1966, 89

19. Barbara Rose: "Looking at American Sculpture", *Artforum,* 3, February 1965, 34

20. Hilton Kramer: "Display of Judd Art Defines an Attitude", *The New York Times,* 14 May, 1971, D48

21. *Donald Judd,* 72

22. See Laurie Anderson: "Mary Miss", *Artforum,* Nov 1973; *Mary Miss: Interior Works,* Bell Gallery, University of Rhode Island, Autumn 1981

23. See Nancy Holt: "Sun Tunnels", *Artforum,* April 1977; "Hydra's Head", *Arts Magazine,* January 1975; Ted Castle: "Nancy Holt, Siteseer", *Art in America,* March 1982

24. Philip Dodd: "Machine dreams", *The Independent,* 27 September 1994, 25; Waldemar Januszczak: "Playing with precision", *The Sunday Times,* 9 October 1994, 10, 12; Adrian Serle: "Hitting the High Notes", *The Independent Magazine,* 1 October 1994, 40f

25. See Mina Roustayi: "Getting Under the Skin: Rebecca Horn's Sensibility Machines", *Arts,* May 1989, 58-68; Michael Kimmelman: "A Sculptural Circus of Whips and Suspense", *New York Times,* 23 Sept 1988, C29

26. Moore, in *The Listener,* 1937, quoted in H. Chipp, ed, 595

27. quoted in Hammacher, op.cit., 98

28. Karen Arthurs: *Mermaid,* 1993, wire, beads, acrylic on papier-mache, collection: the artist, *Unicorn,* 1993, wire, beads, acrylic on papier-mache, collection: the artist. See Jeremy Robinson: *The Madonna Glorified: The Paintings of Karen Arthurs and the Exhibition 'Hours of the Virgin',* Crescent Moon 1991

29. Lila Katzen: *Guardian,* 1979, bronze, 35 x 15 x 3ft, private collection, Saudi Collection

30. Alice Aycock: *One Thousand and One Nights in the Mansion of Bliss,* 1983, mixed media, private collection; *The Miraculous Machine in the Garden (Tower of the Winds),* 1983, mixed media, 16ft high, private collection

31. quoted in Wheeler, 285

32. Catherine King: "Feminist Arts", in Frances Bonner *et al,* eds, 185

33. Catherine Elwes: "Floating femininity: a look at performance art by women",

in S. Kent & J. Morreau, eds: *Women's Images of Men*, Pandora Press, 1985, 182

34. quoted in Lucy Lippard, 219; see also Lucy Lippard: "Dinner Party", *Art in America*, April 1980, 122

35. See David Bourdon et al: *Niki de Sant-Phalle: Fantastic Vision*, Nassau County Musem of Fine Art, Rosyln, New York 1987; Jean-Yves Mock: *Niki de Sant-Phalle: Exposition Retrospective,* CGP 1980

36. See Avis Berman: "Nancy Graves", *Art News*, Feb 1986, 57-64; Debra Bricker Balken and Linda Nochlin: *Nancy Graves: Painting, Sculpture, Drawing 1980-5,* Vassar College Art Gallery, Poughkeepsie, 1986; E.A. Carmean *et al: The Sculpture of Nancy Graves*, Fort Worth 1987; Amy Fine Collins and Bradley Collins: "The Sum of the Parts [Nancy Graves]", *Art in America*, 1988, 113-8; L. Cathcart: *Nancy Graves: A Survey 1969-1980,* Albright-Knox Gallery, catalogue, 1981

37. Houshiary, quoted in *Entre el Objeto*, Palacio de Velasquez, Madrid, 1986, 235

38. Lisa Tickner: "Body Politic", op.cit., 239

39. see T. Gouma-Peterson & P. Matthews: "The feminist critique of art history", *The Art Bulletin,* LXIX, 1987, 326-57

40. see Carolee Schneemann: *Interior Scroll, 1975; More than Meat Joy: Complete Performance Works and Selected Writings,* ed Bruce MacPherson, Documentext, New York 1979

41. C. Carr: "Unspeakable Practices, Unnatural Acts", *Village Voice,* 24 June 1986

42. See Anthony Adler: "Dangerous Woman: Karen Finley", *Chicago Reader,* 26 October 1990; Richard Lacayo: "Talented Toiletmouth", Time, 4 June 1990; Miranda Joseph: "Further Finley", *The Drama Review,* Winter 1990, 13; Kay Larson: "Censor Deprivation", *New York,* 6 August 1990; Catherine Schuler: "Spectator Response and Comprehensions: The Problems of Karen Finley's *Constant State of Desire",* *The Drama Review,* Spring 1990, 131-145; Clive Barnes: "Finley's Fury", *New York Post,* 24 July 1990; Tim Page: "Karen Finley's Tantrum, Amid Chocolate", *New York Newsday,* 24 July 1990

43. Mary Duffy: *Cutting the Ties that Bind, 1987; Stories of a Body,* 1990; see Hilary Robinson: "The Subtle Abyss: Sexuality and Body Image in Contemporary Feminist Art", unpublished dissertation, RCA 1987; Mary Duffy: "Cutting the Ties that Bind", *Feminist Art News,* 2:10, 1989, 6-7; Mary Duffy: "Redressing the Balance", *Feminist Art News,* 3:8, 1991

44. Jo Spence and Tim Sheard: *Narratives of Disease;* see Jo Spence: *Putting Myself in the Picture: A Political, Personal and Photographic Autobiography,* Camden Press 1986; Patricia Holland, Jo Spence and Simon Watney, eds: *Photography/ Politics: Two,* Commedia 1986; Darcy Grimaldo Grigsby: "Dilemmas of Visibility: Contemporary Women Artists' Representations of Female Bodies", *Michigan Quarterly Review,* XXIX: 4, Autumn 1990, 584-618. Other artists who have worked in postmodern, feminist modes include Cindy Sherman, Mary Kelly, Marie Yates, Yve Lomax, Martha Rosler, Sutapa Biswas, Mitra Tabrizian, Zarina Bhimji, Mona Hatoum, Lubaina Himid, Barbara Kruger, Jenny Holzer, Rose Garrard, Susan Hiller, Nancy Spero, Rosa Lee and Rachel Whiteread.

3 : The Alchemy of Forms

1. M. A. Guyton said the meteorite was 'like a black hole draining the mind of speculation on earth, space, matter, time.' (1991, 80)

2. Cooke: *Alison Wilding*, 9

3. unpublished interview 24 July 1984, in Cooke, 10

4. Gresty, 1993, 13

5. Wilding, in Gresty, 13

6. Pierluigi de Vecchi, in Piero della Francesca: *The Complete Paintings*, Penguin 1967/85, 98

7. Kenneth Clark, *Piero della Francesca*, Phaidon 1969, 59

8. Marina Warner, *Alone Of All Her Sex: The Myth and Cult of the Virgin Mary*, Picador 1985, 274

9. see Roderick Coyne

4 : Relationships of Nurturance

1. Mary Beaumont writes: '[m]ystery is...an integral part of Alison Wilding's sculpture, which resists any attempt at literal interpretation.' (77)

2. Cooke writes: 'The sense of a nicely calculated equipoise is a subtle ploy aimed at reinforcing the sense of self-sufficiency and composure that Wilding constantly seeks.' (Cooke, 11)

3. Greg Hilty: *Recent British Sculpture*, Arts Council 1993, 38

4. see Alison Wilding's *Untitled*, 1980

5. Mary Rose Beaumont: 'Mystery is also an integral part of Alison Wilding's sculptures which resists any attempt at literal interpretation. It is concerned with femaleness, which is emphatically not to do with feminism, but rather with what it is like to be a woman.' Beaumont, 77

6. see Lynne Cooke: *Alison Wilding*, Arts Council 1985; L. Biggs: *Between Object and Image*, British Council 1986; Wendy Beckett, 116; Terry A. Neff, 43-45

7. Michael Maier: *Atalanta fugiens*, in H.M.E. de Jong, Leiden 1969

8. Jean Fisher: *On the Margins of Forgetfulness*, Lissom Gallery/ Renaissance Society Publications 1987

9. Rosa Lee: "Resisting amnesia: feminism, painting and postmodernism", *Feminist Review*, 26, 1987, 24

10. Jon Roberts' words, 1990, 175; Peter Gidal, "Fugitive theses are Therese Oulton's *The Passions no. 6* and the *Metals* Paintings", Gimpel Fils Publications 1984

5 : The Sculpture of Embrace: Eroticism in Alison Wilding's Work

1. Wilding, quoted in Wendy Beckett, 116

2. Wilding, statement in *Entre el objecto y la imagen*, Palacio de Velasquez, Parque de Retiro, Madrid, 1986, 236

3. Wilding has said her work made in Cornwall would not be about the 'spirit of

the place' or about 'being there'. The atmosphere of Cornwall is powerful, though, and inevitably seeped into her work.

6 : Alison Wilding and Feminism

1 Irigaray: "Ce sexe qui n'en est pas un", in *Ce sexe qui n'en est pas un*, Minuit, Paris, 1977, and in Marks & Courtivron, eds, 103; see also: Jane Gallop: " *Quand nos levres s'ecrivent:* Irigaray's body politic", Romantic Review, 74, 77-83; Elizabeth Grosz: "Philosophy, subjectivity and the body", in Carole Pateman & Elizabeth Grosz, eds: *Feminist Challenges,* Allen & Unwin, Sydney 1986, 125-43
2 Monique Plaza: ""Phallomorphic power" and the psychology of "woman"", *Ideology and Consciousness,* 4, Autumn 1978, 32
3 Other feminists who have crticized the 'vagino-centric' nature of French feminism include Janet Sayers, *Biologica Politics,* 131; Donna C. Stanton in Miller, 1986, 157-182; Jane Gallop, in Miller, 1986,140; Still & Worton,1993, 60
4 '[women] are already elsewhere than in the discursive machinery where you claim to take them by surprise. They have turned back within themselves, which does not mean the same thing as 'within yourself'. They do not experience the same interiority that you do and which perhaps you mistakenly presume they share.' Irigaray: *Ce sexe qui n'en est pas un,* Minuit, Paris 1977, 28-29
5 Luce Irigaray: "La difference sexuelle", *Ethiope de la difference sexuelle,* Minuit, Paris, 1984, and in Toril Moi, ed: French Feminist Thought, 128
6 Some feminists have criticized French feminists' insistence on the womb and labia, ignoring the clitoris, the organ of 'pure pleasure'. Sayers, 131; Naomi Schor: *Breaking the Chain: Women, Theory and French Realist Fiction,* New York 1985; Still, 1993, 32
7 'If we define female subjectivity through universal biological/ libidinal givens [writes Ann Rosalind Jones}, what happens to the project of changing the world in feminist directions? Further, is women's sexuality so monolithic that shared, typical femininity does justice to it? What about variations in class, in race, and in culture among women? About changes over time in one woman's sexuality? (with men, with women, by herself?) How can one libidinal voice – or the two vulval lips so startlingly presented by Irigaray – speak for all women?' Jones: "Writing the Body", in Showalter, ed, 369
8 Some feminists have criticized French feminists' insistence on the womb and labia, ignoring the clitoris, the organ of 'pure pleasure'. Sayers, 131; Naomi Schor: *Breaking the Chain: Women, Theory and French Realist Fiction,* New York 1985; Still, 1993, 32
9 Whitford, 1991, 88
10 Luce Irigaray, "Women's Exile", in Cameron, 1990, 83; and Luce Irigaray: *Speculum of the Other Woman,* tr Gillian C. Gill, Cornell University Press, New York 1985
11 Irigaray: *Speculum de l'autre femme,* Minuit, Paris 1974
12 Cixous, "The Laugh of the Medusa", in Marks, 254
13 Victor Burgin: "Geometry and Abjection", in John Fletcher and Andrew Benjamin, eds, 115-6

Bibliography

William C. Agee: *Don Judd*, Whitney Museum of American Art, New York 1968
—. *The Sculpture of Donald Judd*, Art Museum of South Texas, Corpus Christi 1977
Wayne Andersen: *American Sculpture in Process 1930/ 1970*, New York Graphics
    Society, Boston 1975
Alison Assister & Avedon Carol, eds: *Bad Girls and Dirty Pictures: The Challenge to
    Reclaim Feminism*, Pluto Press 1993:
Gregory Battock, ed: *Idea Art*, Dutton, New York 1973
—. ed: *Minimal Art: A Criticial Anthology*, Dutton, New York 1968
John Beardsley: *Earthworks and Beyond: Contemporary Art in the Landscape*,
    Abbeville Press, New York, 1984
Nicola Bennett, ed: *The British Art Show: Old Allegiances and New Directions
    1979-1984*, Arts Council/ Orbis 1984
Kent C. Bloomert & Charles W. Moore: *Body, Memory and Architecture*, New
    Haven 1977
Frances Bonner, Lizbeth Goodman, Richard Allen, Linda Jones & Catherine King,
    eds: *Imagining Women Cultural Representations and Gender*, Polity Press,
    Cambridge 1992
J. Butler: *Gender Trouble: Feminism and the Subversion of Identity*, Routledge
    1990
—. & J.W. Scott, eds: *Feminists Theorise the Political*, Routledge 1992
Deborah Cameron, ed: *The Feminist Critique of Language: A Reader*, Routledge
    1990
Joseph Campbell: *The Power of Myth*, with Bill Moyers, ed. Betty Sue Flowers,
    Doubleday, New York 1988
Andrew Causey: *Nature as Material: An Exhibition of Sculpture and Photographs
    Purchased For the Arts Council Collection*, Arts Council 1980

Whitney Chadwick: *Women, Art, and Society*, Thames & Hudson 1990

—. *Women Artists and the Surrealist Movement*, Thames & Hudson 1991

Gail Chester & Julienne Dickey, ed: *Feminism and Censorship: The Current Debate*, Prism Press, Bridport, Dorset 1988

Herschel B. Chipp, ed. *Theories of Modern Art*, University Press of California, Los Angeles 1968

Helene Cixous: *A Helene Cixous Reader*, ed. Susan Sellers, Routledge, 1994

—. & Catherine Clement: *The Newly Born Woman*, tr Betsy Wing, Manchester University Press 1986

Frances Colpitt: *Minimal Art: The Critical Perspective*, University of Washington Press, Seattle, 1990

Lynn Cooke: "Between Image and Object: The "New British Sculpture"", in Neff, 1987

—. "Richard Long replies to a critic", *Art Monthly*, 68, July 1983, 20-21

—. *Alison Wilding*, essay by Lynne Cooke, Serpentine Gallery 1985

Joseph Cornell: *Theatre of the Mind: Selected Diaries, Letters and Files*, Thames & Hudson 1994

Roderick Coyne: "Fugue", in *Threshold*, no. 9, National Museum of Contemporary Art, Oslo, 1993

Penelope Curtis: *Modern British Sculpture from the Collection*, Tate Gallery, Liverpool 1988

Richard Deacon: *Casting an Eye*, Cornerhouse, Manchester 1987

Katy Deepwell, ed: *New Feminist Art Criticism*, Manchester University Press, 1995

Paul de Monchaux, Fenella Crichton & Kate Blacker, eds: *The Sculpture Show*, Arts Council of Great Britain 1983

Enno Develing & Lucy Lippard: *Minimal Art*, Stadtische Kunsthalle, Dusseldorf 1969

Georges Duby & Michele Perrot: *Power and Beauty: Images of Women in Art*, Tauris Parke Books, 1989

Andrea Dworkin: *Intercourse*, Arrow 1988

—. *Pornography: Men Possessing Women*, Women's Press 1984

—. *Letters From a War Zone*, Secker & Warburg 1988

Mary Eagleton, ed: *Feminist Literary Criticism*, Longman 1991

—. ed: *Feminist Literary Theory: A Reader*, Blackwell 1986

Hester Eisenstein: *Contemporary Feminist Thought*, Unwin Paperbacks 1984

Mircea Eliade: *Ordeal by Labyrinth*, University of Chicago Press 1984

—. *Symbolism, the Sacred and the Arts*, Crossroad, New York 1985

Johannes Fabricus: *Alchemy: The Medieval Alchemists and Their Royal Art*, Aquarian Press 1989

John Fletcher & Andrew Benjamin, ed: *Abjection, Melancholia and Love: the Work of Julia Kristeva*, Routledge 1990

Penny Florence & Dee Reynolds, eds: *Feminist subjects, mult-media: Cultural methodologies*, Manchester University Press February 1995

Michel Foucault: *The History of Sexuality*, vol. 1, Penguin 1981

—. *The Use of Pleasure: The History of Sexuality*, vol. 2, Penguin 1987

S. Franklin et al, eds: *Off Centre: Feminism and Cultural Studies*, HarperCollins, New York 1992

Marie-Louise von Franz: *The Psychological Meaning of Redemption in Fairy Tales*,

Inner City Books, Toronto 1980

Peter Fuller: *Peter Fuller's Modern Painters: Reflections on British Art,* ed John McDonald, Methuen 1993

Elinor Gadon: *The Once and Future Goddess,* Aquarian Press 1990

Lorraine Gamman & Margaret Marshment, eds: *The Female Gaze: Women as Viewers of Popular Culture,* Women's Press 1988

Margaret Gardner: *Barbara Hepworth,* Salamander Press, Edinburgh 1982

James Gibson: *The Senses Considered as a Perceptual System,* Houghton Mifflin, Boston 1966

Pamela Church Gibson & Roma Gibson, ed: *Dirty Looks: Women, Pornography, Power,* British Film Institute 1993

Marija Gimbutas: *The Language of the Goddess,* Thames & Hudson 1989

Alan Goldsworthy: *Stone,* Viking 1994

—. *Hand to Earth: Andy Goldsworthy, Sculpture, 1976-1990,* Henry Moore Centre for Sculpture, 1990

Robert Goldwater & Marco Treves, eds. *Artists on Art,* John Murray 1975

Clement Greenberg: *Art and Culture,* Beacon Press, Boston 1961

Germaine Greer: *The Obstacle Race: The Fortunes of Women Painters and Their Work,* Secker & Warburg 1979; Picador 1981

Hilary Gresty: B*are: Alison Wilding: Sculptures 1982-1993,* Newlyn Art Gallery, Cornwall 1993

Gabriele Griffin *et al,* eds: *Stirring It: Challenges For Feminism,* Taylor & Francis 1994

Marjorie Allthorpe Guyton: *Alison Wilding: Sculptures 1987-88,* Karsten Schubert 1988

—. "Immersion and Exposure", *Artscribe,* September 1991

—. *Alison Wilding,* Hirschl & Adler Modern, New York 1989

Abraham M. Hammacher: *The Evolution of Modern Sculpture: Tradition and innovation,* Abrams, New York 1969

Adrian Henri: *Environments and Happenings,* Thames & Hudson 1974

Barbara Hepworth: *A Pictorial Autobiography,* Praeger, New York 1970

Greg Hilty: *Recent British Sculpture,* Arts Council 1993

—. *Alison Wilding: Inmmersion/ Exposure,* Tate Gallery, Liverpool 1991

Robert Hobbs: *Robert Smithson: Sculpture,* Cornell University Press, Ithaca 1981

Janet Hobhouse: *The Bride Stripped Bare: The Artist and the Nude in the Twentieth Century,* Cape 1988

Luce Irigaray: *Je, tu, nous: Toward a Culture of Difference,* tr Alison Martin, Routledge, 1993

—. *Thinking the Difference: For a Peaceful Revolution,* Athlone Press, 1994

—. *The Irigaray Reader,* ed Margaret Whitford, Blackwell, Oxford 1991

Mary Jacobus, ed: *Women Writing and Writing About Women,* Croom Helm 1979

Julia Kristeva: *The Kristeva Reader,* ed Toril Moi, Blackwell 1986

—. *Desire in Language: A Semiotic Approach to Literature and Art,* ed Leon Roudiez, tr Thomas Gora, Alice Jardine & Leon Roudiez, Blackwell 1982

Jacques Lacan and the E*cole Freudienne: Feminine Sexuality,* ed. Juliet Mitchell and Jacqueline Rose, Macmillan 1982

Antoinette Le Normand-Romain, Anne Pingeot, Reinhold Hohl, Jean-Luc Daval,

Barbara Rose: *Sculpture: The Adventure of Modern Sculpture in the Nineteenth and Twentieth Centuries*, Skira, Geneva, 1986

Jeremy Levinson: "Alison Wilding", *The British Show*, British Council/ Art Gallery of New South Wales, 1985

Lucy Lippard: *From the Center: feminist essays on women's art*, Dutton, New York 1976

—. *Six Years: The Dematerialization of the Art Object from 1966 to 1972*, Praeger, New York 1973

Richard Long: *Richard Long: In Conversation*, Parts 1 & 2, MW Press, Noordwijk, Holland 1985-6

—. *Old World New World*, Anthony d'Offay 1988

—. *Richard Long*, Hayward Gallery/ Thames & Hudson, London 1992

Edward Lucie-Smith: *Art Today*, Phaidon 1989

—. *Sculpture Since 1945*, Phaidon 1987

Duncan Macmillan: "David Nash: Brancusi Joins the Garden Gang", *Art Monthly*, 65, April 1983, 7-9

Elaine Marks & Isabelle de Courtivron, eds: *New French Feminisms: an Anthology*, Harvester Wheatsheaf 1981

John McEwen: "Alison Wilding: *The Stuff of Metaphor*", in *Transformation; New Sculpture From Britain*, British Council 1983, 52-59

Allan McPherson: "David Nash: interviewed by Allan McPherson", *Artscribe*, 12, June 1978, 30-34

Ursula Meyer: *Conceptual Art*, Dutton, New York 1972

Nancy Miller, ed: *The Poetics of Gender*, New York, 1986

Toril Moi: *Sexual/ Textual Politics: Feminist Literary Theory*, Routledge 1988

—. ed: *French Feminist Thought: A Reader*, Blackwell, Oxford 1987

J. Morland: *New Milestones: Sculpture, Community and the Land*, Common Ground 1988

Stuart Morris: "A Rhetoric of Silence: Redefinitions of Sculpture in the 1960s and 1970s", in Nairne & Serota, 198

Sandy Nairne & Nicholas Serota: *British Sculpture in the Twentieth Century*, Whitechapel Art Gallery 1981

Terry A. Neff, ed: *A Quiet Revolution: British Sculpture Since 1965*, Thames & Hudson 1987

Michael Newman: "New Sculpture in Britain", *Art in America*, September 1982

Andreas C. Papadakis, ed: *The New Romantics*, Art & Design (vol 4 11/12), Academy Group 1988

—. ed: *British and American Art: The Uneasy Dialectic*, Art & Design (vol 3 9/10, Academy Group 1987

—. ed: *Abstract Art and the Rediscovery of the Spiritual*, Art & Design (vol 3 5/6), Academy Group 1987

Rozsika Parker & Griselda Pollock: *Old Mistresses: Women, Art and Ideology*, Routledge & Kegan Paul 1981

Karen Petersen & J.J. Wilson: *Women Artists: Recognition and Reappraisal from the Early Middle Ages to the Twentieth Century*, Women's Press, 1978

Griselda Pollock: *Vision and Difference: femininity, feminism and histories of art*, Routledge 1988

H.L. Radtke & H.J. Stam, eds: *Gender and Power*, Sage 1994

Janice Radway: *Reading the Romance: Feminism and the Representation of Women in Popular Culture*, University of North Carolina Press, Chapel Hill 1984

Brian Redhead: *The Inspiration of Landscape: Artists in National Parks*, Phaidon 1989

J.L. Reich: "Genderfuck: The Law of the Dildo", *Discourse: Journal of Theoretical Studies in Media and Culture*, vol. 15, no. 1, 1992, 112-127

John Roberts: *Postmodernism, Politics and Art*, Manchester University Press 1990

Marianne Ryan, ed: *Gravity and Grace: The Changing Condition of Sculpture 1965-1975*, Hayward Gallery 1993

Janet Sayers: *Biological Politics*, London 1982

Eric Shanes: *Constantin Brancusi*, Abbeville, New York 1989

Ruth Sherry: *Studying Women's Writings: An Introduction*, Edward Arnold 1988

Elaine Showalter, ed: *The New Feminist Criticism*, Virago 1986

—. ed: *Speaking of Gender*, Routledge 1989

—. *Sexual Anarchy: Gender and Culture at the Fin de Siecle*, Virago 1992

Monica Sjoo & Barbara Mor: *The Great Cosmic Mother*, Harper & Row, San Francisco 1987

David Smith: *Sculpture and Drawings*, ed Jorn Merkert, Prestel-Verlag, Munich 1986

Robert Smithson: *The Writings of Robert Smithson*, ed Nancy Holt, New York University Press, New York 1979

Alan Sonfist, ed: *Art in the Land: A Critical Anthology of Environmental Art*, Dutton, New York 1983

Nikos Stangos, ed: *Concepts of Modern Art*, Thames & Hudson 1981

Judith Still & Michael Worton, eds: *Textuality and Sexuality: Reading Theories and Practices*, Manchester University Press 1993

W.J. Strachan: *Open Air Sculpture in Britain*, Zwemmer 1984

William Tucker: *The Language of Sculpture*, Thames & Hudson 1974

Daniel Wheeler: *Art Since Mid-Century: 1945 to the Present*, Thames & Hudson 1991

Lawrence Weiner: *Lawrence Weiner, Works*, Anatol AV und Filmprouktion Hamburg 1977

Margaret Whitford: *Luce Irigaray: Philosophy of the Feminine*, Routledge 1991

Alison Wilding: *Alison Wilding*, with Michael Tooby, Tate Gallery, St Ives 1994

—. *Alison Wilding: Inmmersion/ Exposure*, Tate Gallery, Liverpool 1991

—. *Entre el objeto y la imagen*, Palacio de Velazquez, Parque de Retiro, Madrid, 1986

Judith Williamson: *Consuming Passion: The Dynamics of Popular Culture*, Marion Boyars 1986

Mara R. Witzling, ed: *Voicing Our Visions: Writing by Women Artists*, Women's Press 1992

Gerard Woods et al, eds: *Art Without Boundaries*, Thames & Hudson 1972

Gray Woods: *Alison Wilding: Sculptures*, Karsten Schubert, 1987

THE ART OF
ANDY GOLDSWORTHY

COMPLETE WORKS: SPECIAL EDITION
(PAPERBACK and HARDBACK)

by William Malpas

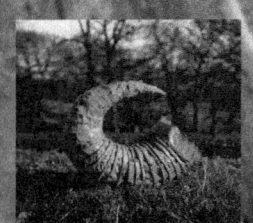

A new, special edition of the study of the contemporary British sculptor, Andy Goldsworthy, including a new introduction, new bibliography and many new illustrations.

This is the most comprehensive, up-to-date, well-researched and in-depth account of Goldsworthy's art available anywhere.

Andy Goldsworthy makes land art. His sculpture is a sensitive, intuitive response to nature, light, time, growth, the seasons and the earth. Goldsworthy's environmental art is becoming ever more popular: 1993's art book *Stone* was a bestseller; the press raved about Goldsworthy taking over a number of London West End art galleries in 1994; during 1995 Goldsworthy designed a set of Royal Mail stamps and had a show at the British Museum. Malpas surveys all of Goldsworthy's art, and analyzes his relation with other land artists such as Robert Smithson, Walter de Maria, Richard Long and David Nash, and his place in the contemporary British art scene.

The Art of Andy Goldsworthy discusses all of Goldsworthy's important and recent exhibitions and books, including the *Sheepfolds* project; the TV documentaries; *Wood* (1996); the New York Holocaust memorial (2003); and Goldsworthy's collaboration on a dance performance.

Illustrations: 70 b/w, 1 colour. 330 pages. New, special, 2nd edition. Publisher: Crescent Moon Publishing. Distributor: Gardners Books.

ISBN 1-86171-059-3 (9781861710598) (Paperback) £25.00 / $44.00

ISBN 1-86171-080-1 (9781861710802) (Hardback) £60.00 / $105.00

ANDY GOLDSWORTHY IN CLOSE-UP

SPECIAL EDITION (HARDBACK and PAPERBACK)

by William Malpas

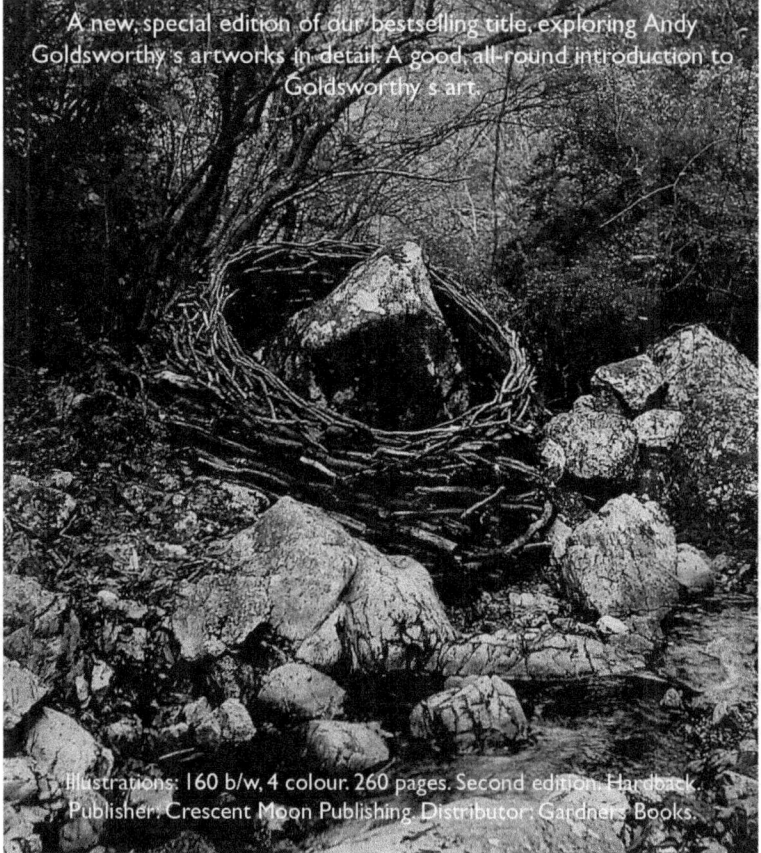

A new, special edition of our bestselling title, exploring Andy Goldsworthy's artworks in detail. A good, all-round introduction to Goldsworthy's art.

Illustrations: 160 b/w, 4 colour. 260 pages. Second edition. Hardback. Publisher: Crescent Moon Publishing. Distributor: Gardner's Books.

ISBN 1-86171-094-1 (9781861710949) (Hbk) £60.00 / $105.00

ISBN 1-86171-091-7 (9781861710919) (Pbk) £25.00 / $44.00

Available from bookstores. amazon.com, play.com, tesco.com, and other web-sites.
In the United States from Baker & Taylor, (800) 7753760 or (800) 7751100 or (908) 5417062. electser@btol.com or btinfo@btol.com.

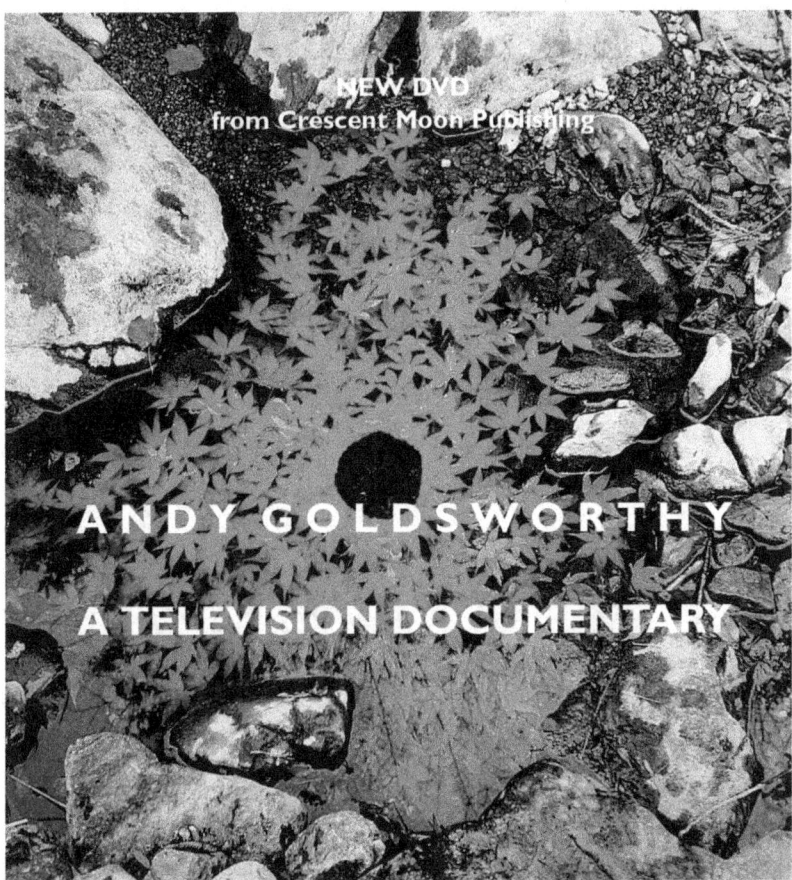

NEW DVD
from Crescent Moon Publishing

ANDY GOLDSWORTHY

A TELEVISION DOCUMENTARY

Andy Goldsworthy makes land art. His sculpture is a sensitive, intuitive response to nature, light, time, growth, the seasons and the earth. Goldsworthy's environmental art is becoming ever more popular: his art books are bestsellers; he has exhibited around the world; important and recent exhibitions include the Sheepfolds project; the Washington installation (2005); Passage (2004); the New York Holocaust memorial (2003); and a collaboration on a dance performance.

This video documentary surveys every aspect of Andy Goldsworthy's art, and all of his major works. It also discusses his relation with other land artists such as Robert Smithson, Walter de Maria, Richard Long and David Nash, and his place in the contemporary art scene in the UK.

This is the only TV documentary of its kind available on DVD and video.

EXTRAS

Resources: further reading; complete bibliography of Andy Goldsworthy, and life and work (on DVD-ROM); and weblinks.
Photo library of land artworks.
Extra footage.

55 minutes. PAL and NTSC. Colour. DVD. Multi-region. VHS video.
Stereo. E (Exempt from classification)

ANDY GOLDSWORTHY

TOUCHING NATURE:
SPECIAL EDITION

(PAPERBACK and HARDBACK)

by William Malpas

A new, special and updated edition of our bestselling title, providing
an excellent general introduction to the art of Andy Goldsworthy.

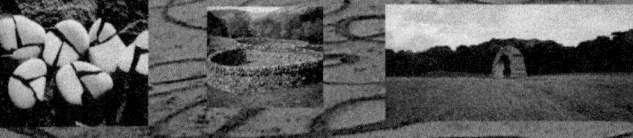

Illustrations: 75 b/w, 2 colour. 354 pages. Third edition. Paperback.

Publisher: Crescent Moon Publishing. Distributor: Gardners Books.

ISBN 1-86171-056-9 (9781861717) (Paperback) £25.00 / $44.00

ISBN 1-86171-087-9 (9781861710871) (Hardback) £60.00 / $105.00

LAND ART

A COMPLETE GUIDE TO LANDSCAPE, ENVIRONMENTAL, EARTHWORKS, NATURE, SCULPTURE AND INSTALLATION ART

by William Malpas

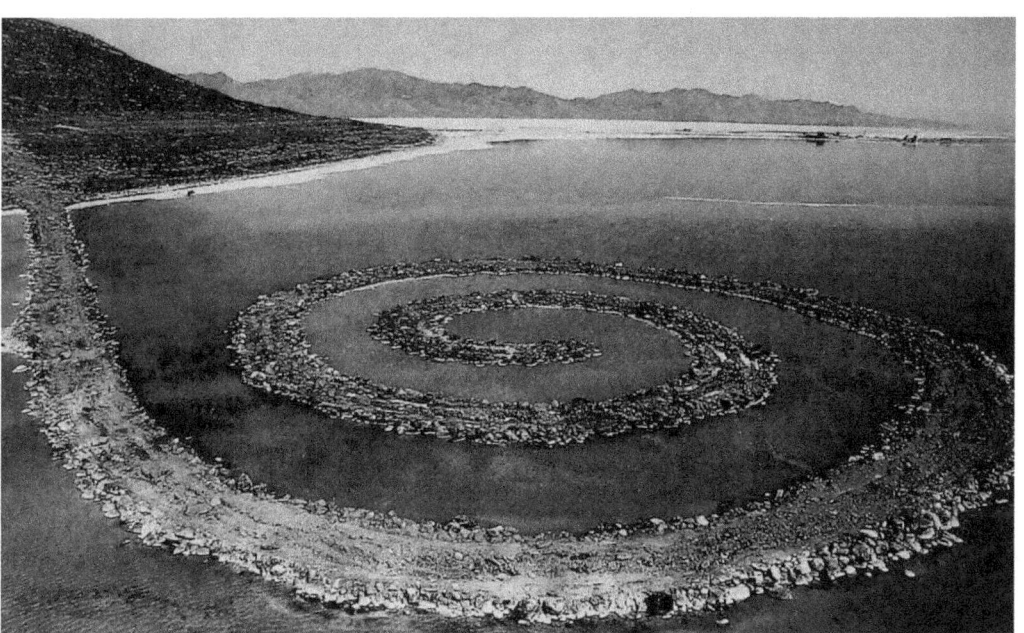

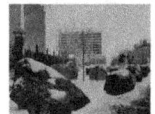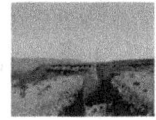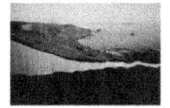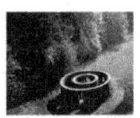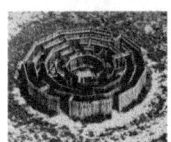

A new, special edition of our popular book on land art.
Chapters on land artists such as Robert Smithson, Walter de Maria, Christo,
Michael Heizer, Richard Long and Andy Goldsworthy.

Illustrations: 35 b/w, 2 colour. 314 pages. First edition. Paperback.

Publisher: Crescent Moon Publishing. Distributor: Gardners Books.

ISBN 1-86171-062-3 (9781861710628) £25.00 / $44.00

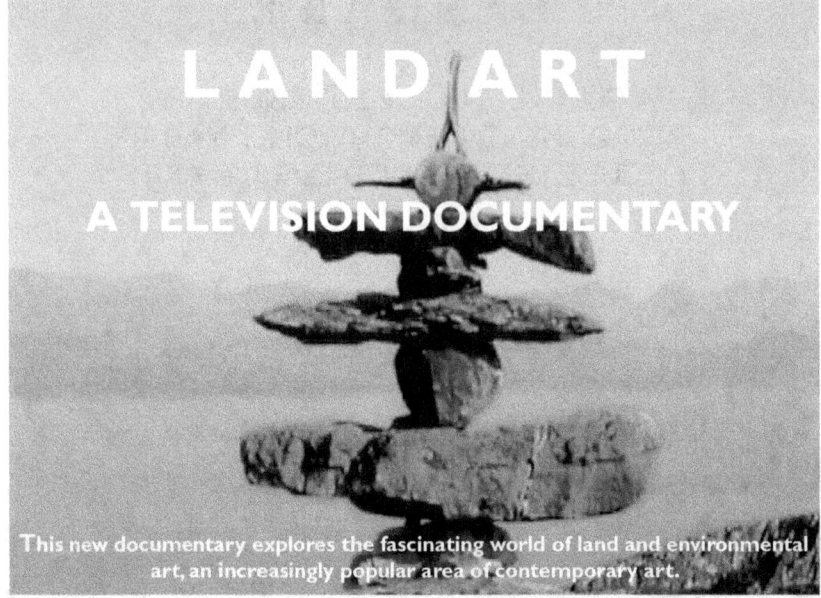

LAND ART

A TELEVISION DOCUMENTARY

This new documentary explores the fascinating world of land and environmental art, an increasingly popular area of contemporary art.

For the land artist, the whole planet is an artist's studio. The land artist ranges over the whole globe. A desert, a beach, a field, a forest becomes a studio, a place of creative activity. Land art is a world of towers and tunnels, stars and scars, pools and pipes, circles and chasms, maps and mazes, stones and cones. This documentary explores all of the major land, environmental and earthwork artists of the past 40 years, including James Turrell and his vast volcano site in Arizona, Michael Heizer's Nevada desert structures, Robert Smithson and his giant spiral, entropic earthworks, Christo's wrapped buildings and islands, Robert Morris's environments, Walter de Maria's Romantic Lightning Field, Hamish Fulton's walks and words, Richard Long and his art of walking, Andy Goldsworthy's natural, spontaneous sculptures, Alice Aycock's mysterious underground mazes, Mary Miss's sunken pools and pavilions, and Nancy Holt and her observatory sculptures.

This is the only TV documentary of its kind available on DVD and video.

EXTRAS

Resources (further reading; complete bibliography of land art (on DVD-ROM); and weblinks).
Photo library of land artworks.

60 minutes. PAL and NTSC. Colour. DVD. Multi-region. VHS video.
Stereo. E (Exempt from classification)

Directed by Jeremy Robinson. Presented by Siena Lloyd.

Producer: Ocean Magic Entertainment. Publisher: Crescent Moon Publishing.

ISBN 1-86171-082-8 (9781861710826) £15.00 / $24.50

LAND ART IN CLOSE-UP

SPECIAL EDITION (PAPERBACK)

by William Malpas

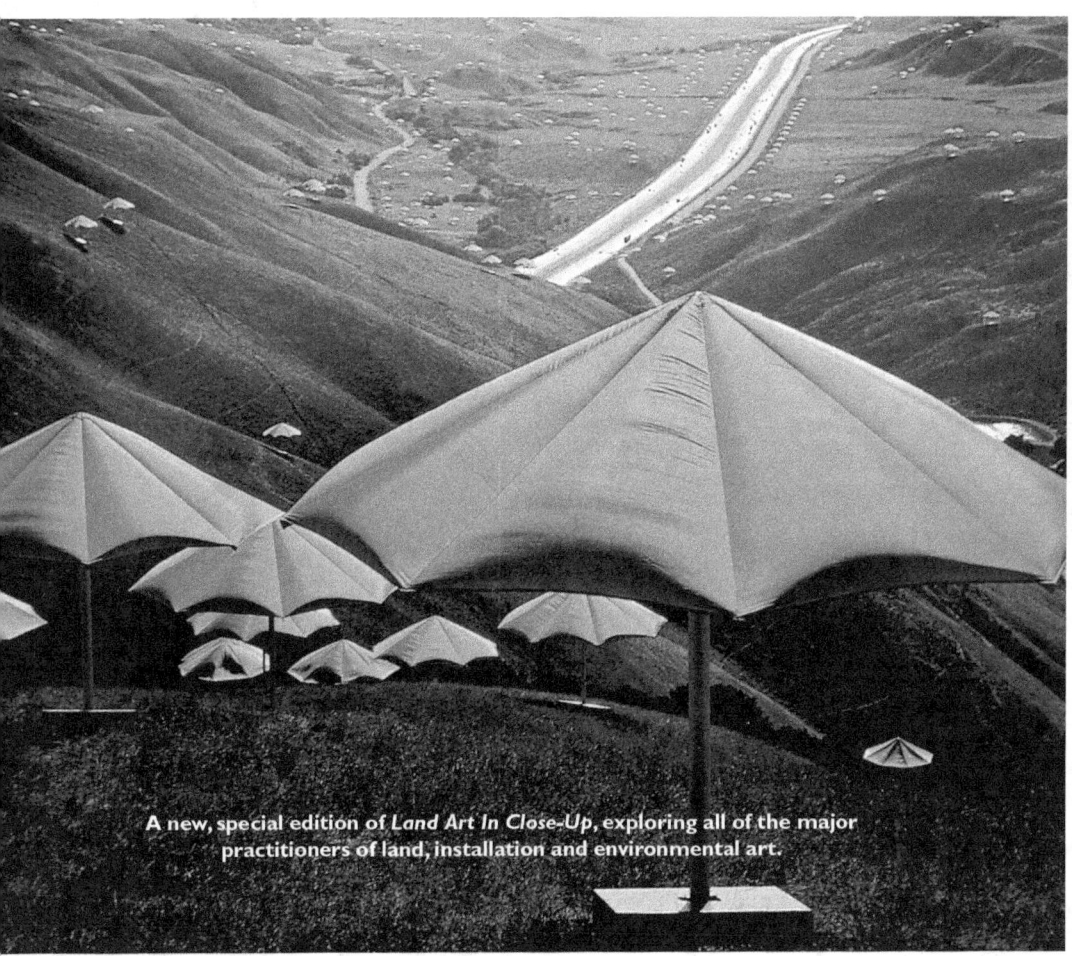

A new, special edition of *Land Art In Close-Up*, exploring all of the major practitioners of land, installation and environmental art.

Illustrations: 161 b/w, 2 colour. 248 pages. Second edition. Paperback.

Publisher: Crescent Moon Publishing. Distributor: Gardners Books.

ISBN 1-86171-092-5 (9781861710925) £25.00 / $44.00

MINIMAL ART AND ARTISTS

FROM THE 1960S AND AFTER

by Laura Garrard

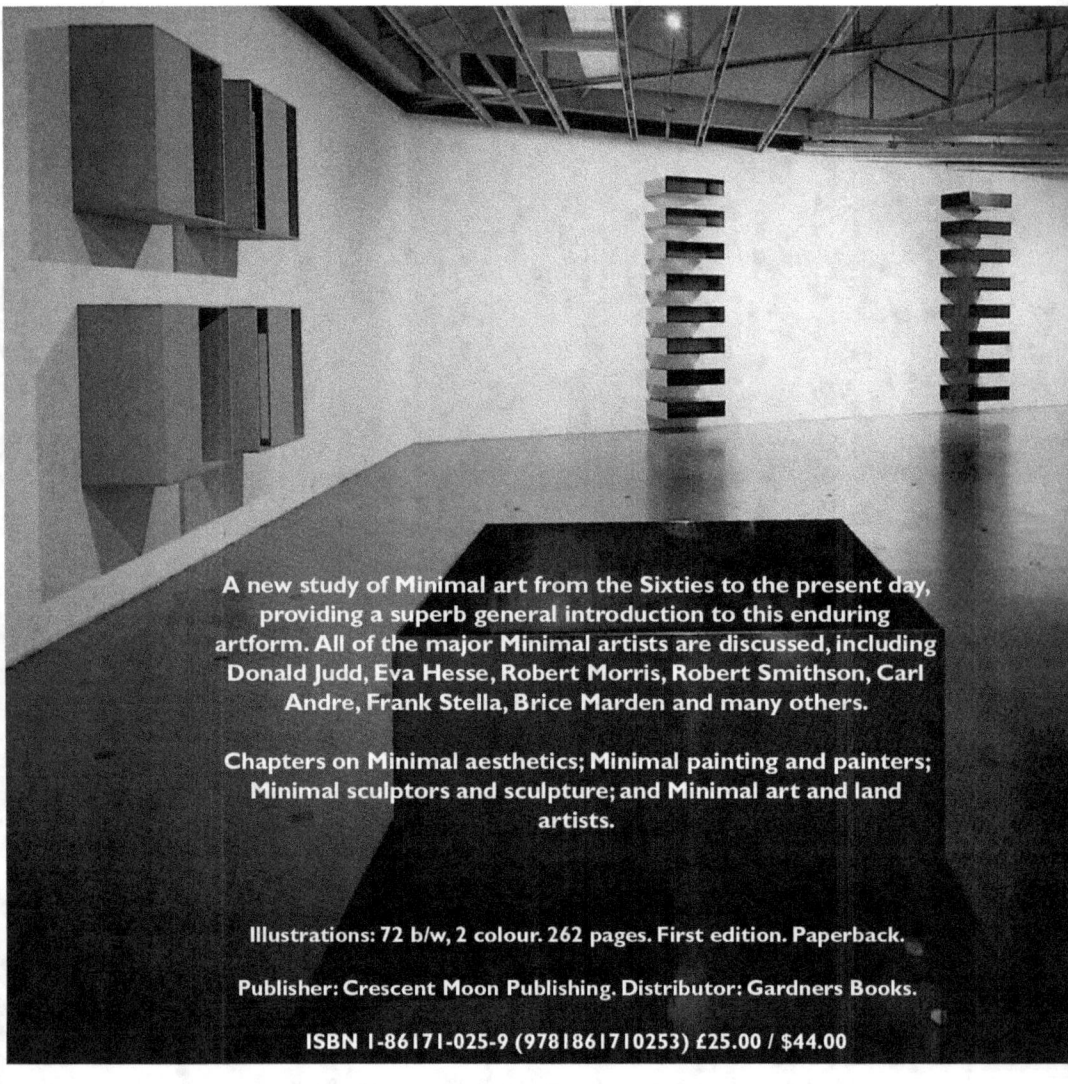

A new study of Minimal art from the Sixties to the present day, providing a superb general introduction to this enduring artform. All of the major Minimal artists are discussed, including Donald Judd, Eva Hesse, Robert Morris, Robert Smithson, Carl Andre, Frank Stella, Brice Marden and many others.

Chapters on Minimal aesthetics; Minimal painting and painters; Minimal sculptors and sculpture; and Minimal art and land artists.

Illustrations: 72 b/w, 2 colour. 262 pages. First edition. Paperback.

Publisher: Crescent Moon Publishing. Distributor: Gardners Books.

ISBN 1-86171-025-9 (9781861710253) £25.00 / $44.00

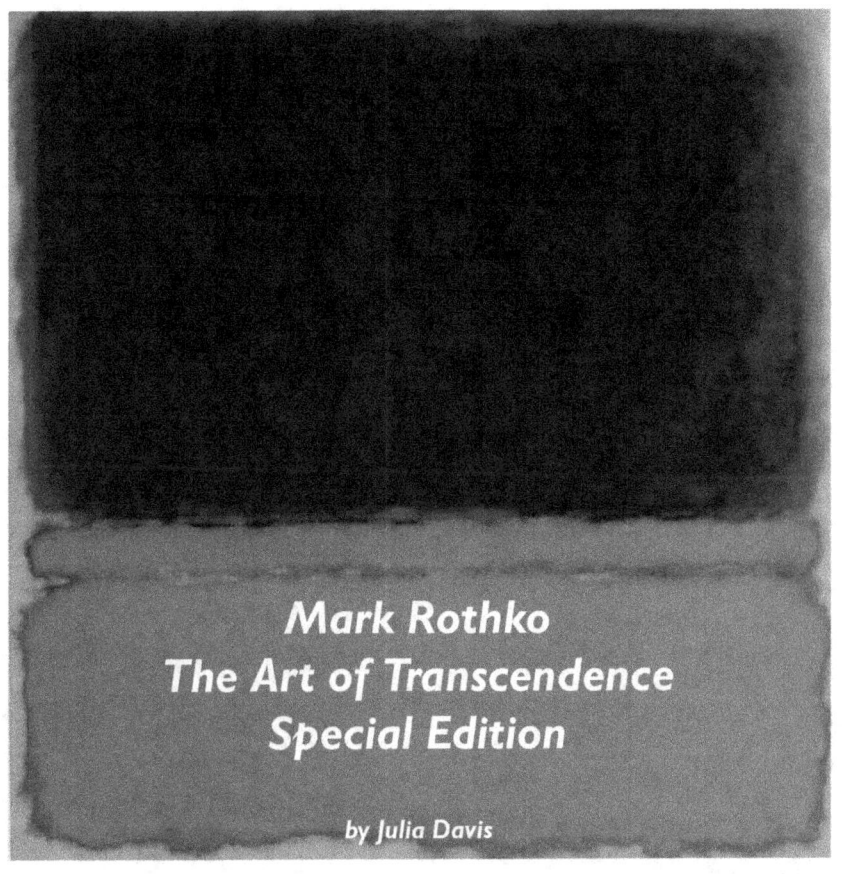

Mark Rothko
The Art of Transcendence
Special Edition

by Julia Davis

Mark Rothko, the American Abstract Expressionist painter, is one of the most widely celebrated of all 20th century artists. His paintings are huge and haunting, marked by themes of tragedy and transcendence. Davis covers Rothko's development from the post-Surrealist semi-figurative works through the radiant canvases of the 1950s, with their floating 'clouds' or 'forms', to the intensity and religiosity of the late mural sequences, the so-called 'Rothko chapels' of Houston, Harvard and the Tate Gallery.

Painters Series   220pp   Bibliography, illustrations, notes   New, 3rd, special edition   ISBN 1-86171-072-0   £14.99 / $26.00

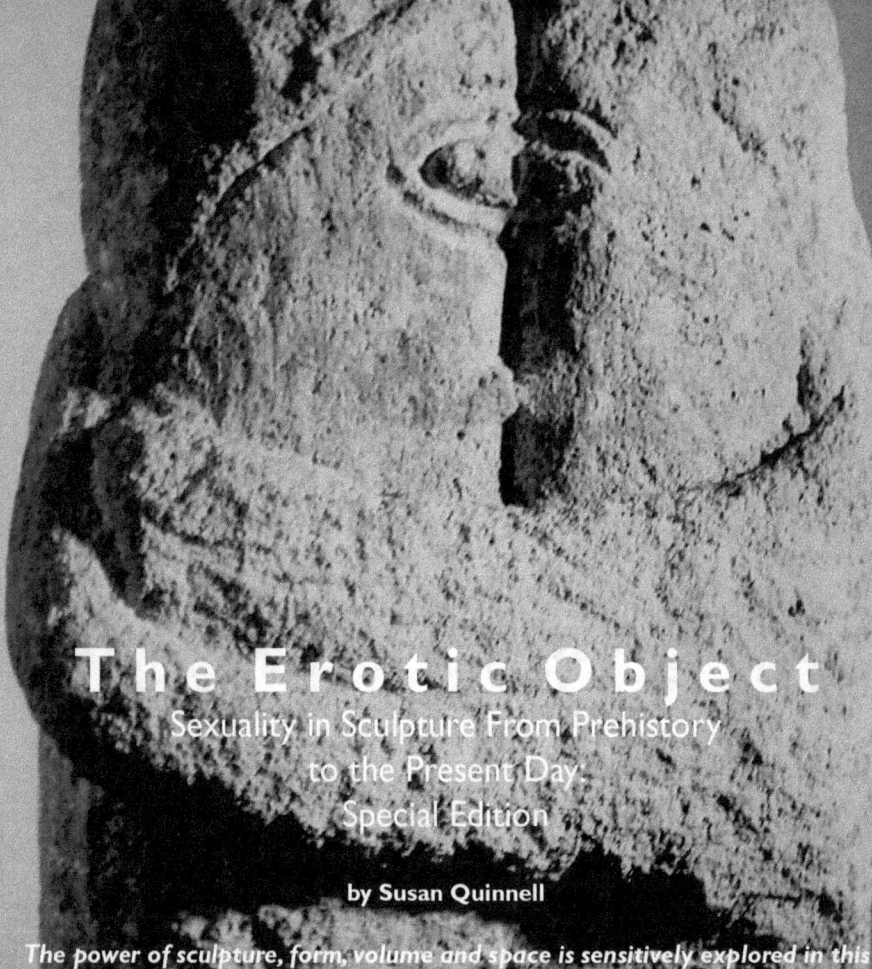

The Erotic Object
Sexuality in Sculpture From Prehistory to the Present Day
Special Edition

by Susan Quinnell

The power of sculpture, form, volume and space is sensitively explored in this wide-ranging study. Featuring discussions of many famous sculptors: Michelangelo, Canova, Rodin, Brancusi, Picasso, Hepworth and Bernini. Many contemporary artists are discussed, including installation and performance artists (Catherine Elwes, Karen Finley, Carolee Schneemann), and women sculptors such as Alice Aycock, Mary Miss, Rebecca Horn, Nancy Graves, Eva Hesse, Kathe Kollwitz and Judy Chicago.
A new special edition, with many new illustrations, a new introduction and bibliography.

(Sculptors Series)   Illustrations, bibliography, notes   326pp.   3rd edition
ISBN 1-86171-069-0   £25.00 / $37.50

THE ART OF
RICHARD LONG

COMPLETE WORKS : SPECIAL EDITION
(HARDBACK and PAPERBACK)

by William Malpas

A new study of the British artist Richard Long, an important contemporary international artist. The most detailed, in-depth exploration of Richard Long's art currently available.

Illustrations: 48 b/w, 2 colour. 439 pages.
First edition. Hardback and paperback editions.

Publisher: Crescent Moon Publishing. Distributor: Gardners Books.

ISBN 1-86171-079-8 (9781861710796) (Hardback) £60.00 / $105.00

ISBN 1-86171-081-X (9781861710819) (Paperback) £25.00 / $44.00

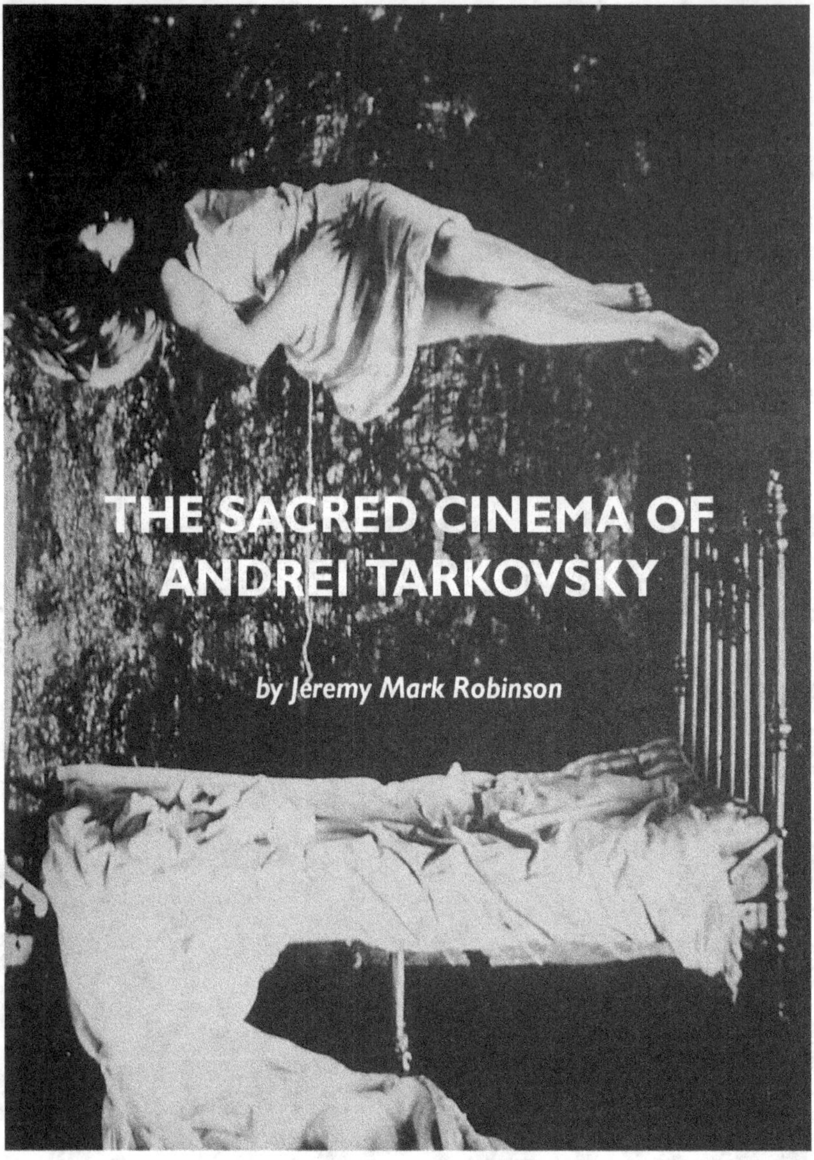

THE SACRED CINEMA OF
ANDREI TARKOVSKY

by Jeremy Mark Robinson

A new study of the Russian filmmaker Andrei Tarkovsky (1932-1986), director of seven feature films, including *Andrei Roublyov, Mirror, Solaris, Stalker* and *The Sacrifice*.

This is one of the most comprehensive and detailed studies of Tarkovsky's cinema available. Every film is explored in depth, with scene-by-scene analyses. All aspects of Tarkovsky's output are critiqued, including editing, camera, staging, script, budget, collaborations, production, sound, music, performance and spirituality. Tarkovsky is placed with a European New Wave tradition of filmmaking, alongside directors like Ingmar Bergman, Carl Theodor Dreyer, Pier Paolo Pasolini and Robert Bresson.

An essential addition to film studies.

Illustrations: 150 b/w, 4 colour. 682 pages. First edition. Hardback.

Publisher: Crescent Moon Publishing. Distributor: Gardners Books.

ISBN 1-86171-096-8 (9781861710963) £60.00 / $105.00

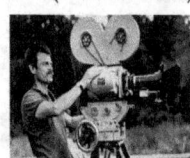

CRESCENT MOON PUBLISHING

ARTS, PAINTING, SCULPTURE

The Art of Andy Goldsworthy: Complete Works(Pbk)
The Art of Andy Goldsworthy: Complete Works (Hbk)
Andy Goldsworthy in Close-Up (Pbk)
Andy Goldsworthy in Close-Up (Hbk)
Land Art: A Complete Guide
Richard Long: The Art of Walking
The Art of Richard Long: Complete Works (Pbk)
The Art of Richard Long: Complete Works (Hbk)
Richard Long in Close-Up
Land Art In the UK
Land Art in Close-Up
Installation Art in Close-Up
Minimal Art and Artists In the 1960s and After
Colourfield Painting
Land Art DVD, TV documentary
Andy Goldsworthy DVD, TV documentary
The Erotic Object: Sexuality in Sculpture From Prehistory to the Present Day
Sex in Art: Pornography and Pleasure in Painting and Sculpture
Postwar Art
Sacred Gardens: The Garden in Myth, Religion and Art
Glorification: Religious Abstraction in Renaissance and 20th Century Art
Early Netherlandish Painting
Leonardo da Vinci
Piero della Francesca
Giovanni Bellini
Fra Angelico: Art and Religion in the Renaissance
Mark Rothko: The Art of Transcendence
Frank Stella: American Abstract Artist
Jasper Johns: Painting By Numbers
Brice Marden
Alison Wilding: The Embrace of Sculpture
Vincent van Gogh: Visionary Landscapes
Eric Gill: Nuptials of God
Constantin Brancusi: Sculpting the Essence of Things
Max Beckmann
Egon Schiele: Sex and Death In Purple Stockings
Delizioso Fotografico Fervore: Works In Process 1
Sacro Cuore: Works In Process 2
The Light Eternal: J.M.W. Turner
The Madonna Glorified: Karen Arthurs

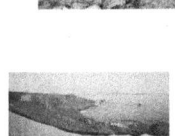
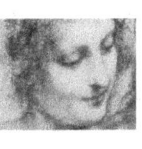
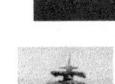
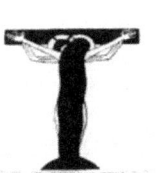
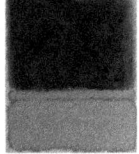
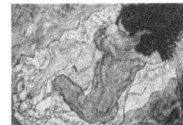

LITERATURE

J.R.R. Tolkien: The Books, The Films, The Whole Cultural Phenomenon
Harry Potter
Sexing Hardy: Thomas Hardy and Feminism
Thomas Hardy's *Tess of the d'Urbervilles*
Thomas Hardy's *Jude the Obscure*
Thomas Hardy: The Tragic Novels
Love and Tragedy: Thomas Hardy
The Poetry of Landscape in Hardy
Wessex Revisited: Thomas Hardy and John Cowper Powys
Wolfgang Iser: Essays
Petrarch, Dante and the Troubadours
Maurice Sendak and the Art of Children's Book Illustration
Andrea Dworkin
Cixous, Irigaray, Kristeva: The *Jouissance* of French Feminism
Julia Kristeva: Art, Love, Melancholy, Philosophy, Semiotics and Psychoanalysis
Hélène Cixous I Love You: The *Jouissance* of Writing
Luce Irigaray: Lips, Kissing, and the Politics of Sexual Difference
Peter Redgrove: Here Comes the Flood
Peter Redgrove: Sex-Magic-Poetry-Cornwall
Lawrence Durrell: Between Love and Death, East and West
Love, Culture & Poetry: Lawrence Durrell
Cavafy: Anatomy of a Soul
German Romantic Poetry: Goethe, Novalis, Heine, Hölderlin, Schlegel, Schiller
Feminism and Shakespeare
Shakespeare: Selected Sonnets
Shakespeare: Love, Poetry & Magic
The Passion of D.H. Lawrence
D.H. Lawrence: Symbolic Landscapes
D.H. Lawrence: Infinite Sensual Violence
Rimbaud: Arthur Rimbaud and the Magic of Poetry
The Ecstasies of John Cowper Powys
Sensualism and Mythology: The Wessex Novels of John Cowper Powys
Amorous Life: John Cowper Powys and the Manifestation of Affectivity (H.W. Fawkner)
Postmodern Powys: New Essays on John Cowper Powys (Joe Boulter)
Rethinking Powys: Critical Essays on John Cowper Powys
Paul Bowles & Bernardo Bertolucci
Rainer Maria Rilke
In the Dim Void: Samuel Beckett
Samuel Beckett Goes into the Silence
André Gide: Fiction and Fervour
Jackie Collins and the Blockbuster Novel
Blinded By Her Light: The Love-Poetry of Robert Graves
The Passion of Colours: Travels In Mediterranean Lands
Poetic Forms
The Dolphin-Boy

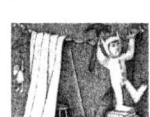

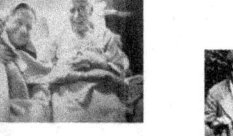
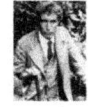

POETRY

The Best of Peter Redgrove's Poetry
Peter Redgrove: Here Comes The Flood
Peter Redgrove: Sex-Magic-Poetry-Cornwall
Ursula Le Guin: Walking In Cornwall
Dante: Selections From the Vita Nuova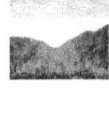
Petrarch, Dante and the Troubadours
William Shakespeare: Selected Sonnets
Blinded By Her Light: The Love-Poetry of Robert Graves
Emily Dickinson: Selected Poems
Emily Brontë: Poems
Thomas Hardy: Selected Poems
Percy Bysshe Shelley: Poems
John Keats: Selected Poems
D.H. Lawrence: Selected Poems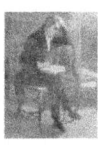
Edmund Spenser: Poems
John Donne: Poems
Henry Vaughan: Poems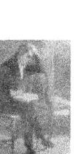
Sir Thomas Wyatt: Poems
Robert Herrick: Selected Poems
Rilke: Space, Essence and Angels in the Poetry of Rainer Maria Rilke
Rainer Maria Rilke: Selected Poems
Friedrich Hölderlin: Selected Poems
Arseny Tarkovsky: Selected Poems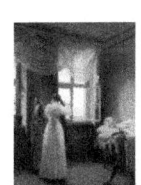
Arthur Rimbaud: Selected Poems
Arthur Rimbaud: A Season in Hell
Arthur Rimbaud and the Magic of Poetry
D.J. Enright: By-Blows
Jeremy Reed: Brigitte's Blue Heart
Jeremy Reed: Claudia Schiffer's Red Shoes
Gorgeous Little Orpheus
Radiance: New Poems
Crescent Moon Book of Nature Poetry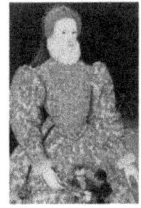
Crescent Moon Book of Love Poetry
Crescent Moon Book of Mystical Poetry
Crescent Moon Book of Elizabethan Love Poetry
Crescent Moon Book of Metaphysical Poetry
Crescent Moon Book of Romantic Poetry
Pagan America: New American Poetry

MEDIA, CINEMA, FEMINISM and CULTURAL STUDIES

J.R.R. Tolkien: The Books, The Films, The Whole Cultural Phenomenon
Harry Potter
Cixous, Irigaray, Kristeva: The *Jouissance* of French Feminism
Julia Kristeva: Art, Love, Melancholy, Philosophy, Semiotics and   Psychoanalysis
Luce Irigaray: Lips, Kissing, and the Politics of Sexual Difference
Hélene Cixous I Love You: The *Jouissance* of Writing
Andrea Dworkin
'Cosmo Woman': The World of Women's Magazines
Women in Pop Music
Discovering the Goddess (Geoffrey Ashe)
The Poetry of Cinema
The Sacred Cinema of Andrei Tarkovsky (Pbk and Hbk)
Paul Bowles & Bernardo Bertolucci
Media Hell: Radio, TV and the Press
An Open Letter to the BBC
Detonation Britain: Nuclear War in the UK
Feminism and Shakespeare
Wild Zones: Pornography, Art and Feminism
Sex in Art: Pornography and Pleasure in Painting and Sculpture
Sexing Hardy: Thomas Hardy and Feminism

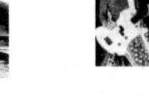
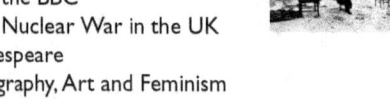
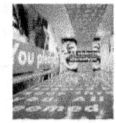
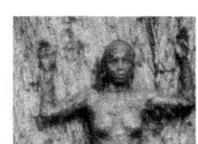
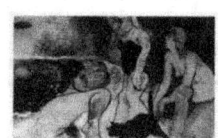
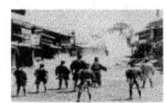
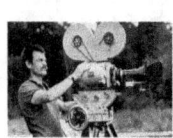

In my view *The Light Eternal* is among the very best of all the material I read on Turner. (Douglas Graham, director of the Turner Museum, Denver, Colorado)

The Light Eternal is a model monograph, an exemplary job. The subject matter of the book is beautifully organised and dead on beam. (Lawrence Durrell)

It is amazing for me to see my work treated with such passion and respect. (Andrea Dworkin)

Sex-Magic-Poetry-Cornwall is a very rich essay... It is like a brightly-lighted box. (Peter Redgrove)

CRESCENT MOON PUBLISHING
P.O. Box 393, Maidstone, Kent, ME14 5XU, United Kingdom.
01622-729593 (UK) 01144-1622-729593 (US) 0044-1622-729593 (other territories)
cresmopub@yahoo.co.uk   www.crescentmoon.org.uk

www.ingramcontent.com/pod-product-compliance
Lightning Source LLC
Chambersburg PA
CBHW071313220526
45468CB00001B/354